Mindfulness Therapy

Beginner's Introduction to Live a Less Stressful Life Through Guided Meditation

(Receive Your Ultimate Desires Using the Law of Attraction)

Rick McCarthy

Published by Rob Miles

© **Rick McCarthy**

All Rights Reserved

Mindfulness Therapy: Beginner's Introduction to Live a Less Stressful Life Through Guided Meditation (Receive Your Ultimate Desires Using the Law of Attraction)

ISBN 978-1-990084-07-2

All rights reserved. No part of this guide may be reproduced in any form without permission in writing from the publisher except in the case of brief quotations embodied in critical articles or reviews.

Legal & Disclaimer

The information contained in this book is not designed to replace or take the place of any form of medicine or professional medical advice. The information in this book has been provided for educational and entertainment purposes only.

The information contained in this book has been compiled from sources deemed reliable, and it is accurate to the best of the Author's knowledge; however, the Author cannot guarantee its accuracy and validity and cannot be held liable for any errors or omissions. Changes are periodically made to this book. You must consult your doctor or get professional medical advice before using any of the suggested remedies, techniques, or information in this book.

Upon using the information contained in this book, you agree to hold harmless the Author from and against any damages, costs, and expenses, including any legal fees potentially resulting from the application of any of the information provided by this guide. This disclaimer applies to any damages or injury caused by the use and application, whether directly or indirectly, of any advice or information presented, whether for breach of contract, tort, negligence, personal injury, criminal intent, or under any other cause of action.

You agree to accept all risks of using the information presented inside this book. You need to consult a professional medical practitioner in order to ensure you are both able and healthy enough to participate in this program.

Table of Contents

INTRODUCTION 1

CHAPTER 1: DEFINING MEDITATION................................. 7

CHAPTER 2: MINDFULNESS MEDITATION 19

CHAPTER 3: BREATHING TECHNIQUES............................. 23

CHAPTER 4: THE PSYCHOLOGICAL BENEFITS OF MEDITATION 31

CHAPTER 5: OBSERVING YOUR THOUGHTS 38

CHAPTER 6: MINDFULNESS: THE ART OF CULTIVATING RESILIENCE 45

CHAPTER 7: MIND MAINTENANCE 51

CHAPTER 8: MINDFULNESS MEDITATION 58

CHAPTER 9: BODY AWARENESS/SCAN MINDFULNESS..... 63

CHAPTER 10: MUSCLE RELAXATION 67

CHAPTER 11: THINKING.. 72

CHAPTER 12: HOW TO MEDITATE: PRACTICAL EXERCISES 93

CHAPTER 13: MINDFULNESS TECHNIQUES 106

CHAPTER 14: PUTTING IT ALL TOGETHER....................... 126

CHAPTER 15: THE PROBLEM OF THE PRESENT 130

CHAPTER 16: DEVELOP YOUR SELF-REGULATION 141

CHAPTER 17: MINDFULNESS MEDITATION TO DEAL WITH ANXIETY 160

CHAPTER 18: A STEP FORWARD TO A HAPPIER LIFE 166

CONCLUSION 180

Introduction

Everything you've ever wanted begins with mindfulness.
We want to sleep more and have sweet dreams. We want to do the difficult things, like compete or perform or present, and feel more comfortable. We want to have more good days.
But we get stuck on the mechanics.
Intuitively, at least some of the time, we already know we're supposed to pay attention to the moment.
But how?
How often?
We can't really put our finger on what separates the bad days from the ones we wish would never end. We don't know what the first mindful step looks like. So we guess.
We don't have to guess anymore.
What we now know thanks to historical and empirical evidence is that the doors to the life we really want are in our own body

and brain. The great teachers, the highest achievers, and the happiest people have already figured it out. In the last twenty years, scientific discoveries about our brains have proven a clear truth you can practice and master: mindfulness determines what happens next.

Let's have a taste.

Over the next thirty seconds, identify as many sounds as you can hear.

Close your eyes and listen.

How many could you discern?

I notice my computer's fan whirling. The dishwasher downstairs is humming. A saw screeches from the construction next door. A bird sings (God, I love it when I truly hear the birds sing). A boat's horn sounds in the distance.

For you, right now, how did it feel to just listen? Stressful? Surprisingly calm? Did other thoughts intrude? Was it a break from the day?

What about your breath? Did you notice it? In the past, when I would just listen, I didn't. I was so focused on the sounds outside myself that I never heard my own presence.

And that's not wrong. The old part of our brains isn't concerned with being. It trusts that your autonomic systems like respiration will happen without you consciously noticing. The old part of your brain wants you to survive. It has an alarm, technically called the amygdala, that keeps us alert and out of danger. The alarm's primary concern is bears.

But wait: Any bears around you right now? The man snoring next to you on the plane may feel like a bear. Your neighbor's dog that wakes you up every morning may feel like a bear. Your deadlines, to-do list, annoying people, unfulfilled goals and nagging aches and pains may feel like bears.

So let's just make sure one more time: Any bears?

The problem is our alarms cannot tell the difference between a real threat to our lives and a perceived threat that isn't truly a problem. That's why we can't sleep. That's what makes us feel so anxious and depressed. That's why we struggle to be ourselves.

When you feel stress and the emotions like fear and worry that go with it, neuroscience has shown it is because your alarm is firing. The bear and the snoring seat mate cause the same chemicals to pour into your blood stream. Obviously the bear and the irritation will cause different levels of stress, but unchecked, the things that annoy us eventually fill our bodies with the same level of hormones caused by sudden danger.

We used to think something was wrong with us when we felt like melting down (or did). It turns out, when you feel stress and its cohort of irritating emotions and ruminations, it means something is entirely right.

Your old brain is making sure you stay alive. It wants your DNA to carry on. Your genetic imperative can't prosper if you are literally something's lunch. We have so much more to pay attention to these days, and the surges of stress caused by social media, the global economy, and too-packed-to-the-brim schedules are natural.

Pause and listen again, but this time pick one sound to focus on.

Did you enjoy the rhythm, the hum or the melody of that which you chose to notice?

As you just listened, you were here. Now. Free. Your past wasn't haunting you. Your future wasn't a worry.

What you may not know is that you just intentionally did something to your brain that is crucial for better sleep, managing stress, and feeling happy. Even if you're in the middle of crazy times, when you focus on one thing that you choose, fMRI studies show it turns down your alarm. Your alarm can be a painful, persistent problem; or, you can learn to make it an ally.

Too many of us are swept away by the constant triggers to our brain's alarm. You won't be when you know how to:

1) Seize time away
2) Recognize the mindful teachers in your life
3) Explain the science of a mindful brain
4) Measure stress
5) Experiment with the different forms of mindfulness
6) Decide which practice is right for you today
7) Commit to a regular practice that feels natural
8) Define the first goal in every situation
9) Savor the mindful you

Chapter 1: Defining Meditation

There are a number of things in life that are way beyond human control. It is, however, possible to take full responsibility of our state of mind. It is also possible to change our minds for the better. Based on the teachings of Buddhism, this is one of the most important things that we can do to ourselves. It is the only known antidote to all the personal sorrows that we might be undergoing, as well as to the hatreds, fears, and anxieties that tend to beset the human condition.

Meditation is basically a means of changing the mind. It can also be defined as the techniques that develop and encourage concentration, emotional positivity, clarity, and calm observation of the real nature of things. By engaging with a given practice of meditation, you will be able to learn the habits and patterns of the mind. In return, the practice provides a means to cultivate more positive and new ways of staying healthy. These focused and nourished state of mind can deepen in energized and peaceful states of mind with patience and regular work. It is also important to note that such experiences can also bear a transformative effect and can even lead to a new understanding of life.

Basically, meditation is just learning to work with the mind. According to the definition offered by The Cambridge dictionary, meditation can be defined as the act of giving your full attention to just one thing, as a religious activity or a way of becoming relaxed and calm. Therefore, meditation can include pondering, relaxing, focusing, or the expression of all these just as the famous Marcus Aurelius meditations.

Before going to the extremes of inquiring about what meditation is, it would also be very important to know what isn't. It is not all about zoning out, mind control or even encountering earth-shattering experiences. As a spiritual practice, meditation is more about coordinating with the mind, as well as training in awareness. Working with the mind in a simple manner will definitely lead to a great sense of attractiveness, calm, presence, as well as an increase in human valued qualities like patience and empathy.

As noted at the beginning of this eBook, a lot of things are way beyond our control, but it is still so easy to have great control over all our actions and even how we respond to the situations that we bump in. To be able to do this, it is important to cultivate awareness of how the mind operates as well as the ability to maintain a great focus. There is nothing that cultivates awareness as meditation.

According to Buddhism, taking care of the mind is one of the most important human undertakings. In addition to that, it also teaches us that taking full charge of the mind is not all about controlling it. It is basically about giving ourselves the means to be able to connect with the innate qualities of the mind.

These qualities include creativity, goodness, as well as spaciousness. It does that to enable the natural light of the mind to outshine the shadows of disturbing emotions and confusion. A free mind will be able to find its own peace. As Suzuki Roshi, the great Zen master once put it, to offer your cow or sheep a huge spacious meadow is the best way of controlling them.

Take time to consider this – All the things that we experience are experienced solely by the mind. In the absence of all that, we would just be machines. Our sorrows and joys, memories, knowledge, love, anger, artistic abilities and any other thing are experienced through the mind. The question that arises is the amount of time that we devote to properly know this mind, and even train it. Meditation is essentially just that; as opposed to just focusing on the external world as we always do. All we are doing is to befriend the mind and training it to be more relaxed and aware.

And So, What is Meditation?

We need to get back to the beginning: meditation is basically awareness. Each time we meditate, we are getting dedicating a particular amount of effort and time to being as mindful as we are able to. To be able to do this, we always opt for a meditation object – for instance, the breath – and then pay great attention to it. We may opt to sit on a chair or a cushion, remaining still and upright, and just settle our mind on the breath. Oftentimes, we realize that the mind does not just stay put as it is supposed to, and the next thing we do is start imagining telling a workmate that we are thinking of them or even booking a flight to a dream city. And how did that just occurred? That is what the mind is. It is entirely creative and desires to make itself clearly heard at all times.

Offering it space to express itself is the initial step to getting to know it and even learning to harness its power. Each time we realize that we have wandered from our breath, we always invite the mind to get back in a firm and gentle manner. This is what can be defined as the practice of being mindful. The mind will catch on as time moves on. We shall have discovered the richness and peace of remaining present, and it even gets hard and harder to easily pulls away. It can just be compared to those video clips of cows that spend most of their winter in the barn being let out into a spring pastures for the very first time.

They excitedly move, graze and sniff as they immensely enjoy themselves, and finally, the experience wears off and they eventually contentedly ruminate and settle down. Some of the lessons that meditation teaches us are that both presence and contentedness are the real keys to happiness. They remain so even if the society attempts to convince us that the latest technology gadgets are the key.

According to a philosopher and a highly regarded master of meditation, Trinlay Rinpoche, our happiness does not come from the material pursuits or the external factors. The main source of our happiness comes right from within us. Each time we put meditation into practice, our mind is able to learn how to be able to access the wealth of qualities that are already within us. And each time we are able to access the most essential qualities of compassion and goodness, we will naturally offer them expression in the world that is around us. That is what meditation is used for.

How Attention Changes our Brains

During mindfulness meditation, we are required to always use our attention. By doing that, we will be training our brains to be more connected to the present world. This has a great effect of enabling ourselves to see what is really going on, without really getting caught in our opinion of the circumstance at hand.

Mediation has grown to be very popular, and at times, we might ask the main reason behind it. First of all, it is important to note that the brain anatomy that we tap from our parents will tell the real landscape upon which the empire of our brains will be anchored. There are certain personal tendencies that we inherit from our parents such as the area's natural resources, the weather patterns, and others.

These tendencies are largely predetermined, but can still be deteriorated or nurtured by the habits that we have. It is also very imperative to note that the brain's landscape-anatomy will also determine the kind of skills that we can perform best, and the habits that become automatic, but there is still a twist to this main story.

Neuroscientists have also discovered that where we direct our attention and not just the conditions alone determine the specific areas that should be developed and redeveloped. Our attention will always change the anatomy – it can just be compared to the construction crew and land developer all under one roof. Our brain's developed landscape will determine how it operates. The ability to alter our brains' landscape and regulate how the minds will work is what is known as neuroplasticity.

We are willingly, constantly, changing the structure of our most fascinating organ as we move our attention from one place to another. At any point in time, we start commanding areas that should be reorganized and order the direction that the mind will take thereafter. Note that all our mental exercises will have this kind of effect, and the areas that they influence will be based on the skills that we are applying. This kind of certainty adds a particular level of complexity to the entire "nurture or nature" question of how our talents and personalities are shaped.

Science has also discovered that once a particular skill has been done without the necessary attention, the brain will cease shaping the areas. The main work of our brain is to figure out that part of our empire is just working right and places its resources somewhere else. Walking is one of the best examples, but after we have walked so well, we can practically ignore that we are doing it, and the complex movements will not change that much. Even though we constantly practice to walk better, we rarely achieve it. From time to time, we all roll our ankles and trip, but unless we have a serious injury our brains will stick with what had previously worked.

It is beneficial to develop our concentration via meditation, always focusing and refocusing our main attention. Through meditation, we learn to engage the brain areas that are not so much used in our day-to-day life. Even though each technique will have special effects, all types of meditation posses the common theme of gradually quieting our minds and enabling us to feel a connection to the current moment. This has the effect of allowing ourselves to see what is really going on, without getting caught in the opinion of the situation.

What we disengage from in the current moment is full of fantasies, worries, memories, and this is one of the reasons why several forms of meditation can assist in alleviating the symptoms of anxiety and depression. Even though mindfulness meditation works on a number of brain centers as the one seen with anti-depressants, we are not very certain if the effects rise from the very chemical mechanism.

Each form of meditation starts the training with certain mention of breath and focus. Every person who is alive breathes. It does not really matter the language that we speak or the kind of religion that we follow, breathing is a common denominator and familiar to all of us.

Chapter 2: Mindfulness Meditation

Mindfulness meditation is based, as it was already mentioned, on Buddhist practices. Practitioners of mindfulness meditation are taught first of all how to be mindful, concentrating their attention on the present. They learn how to develop a strong mind, assuming the necessary skills for keeping emotions separate from actual experiences; in this way, the next time they are confronted with a similar situation, they will be to provide a mindful response.

There are different positions that one can assume during the meditation process but one of the most common ones is sitting relaxed, with the eyes closed and the legs crossed, the back maintaining however a straight position. One can assume this position on a chair or on the floor, diverting all of his or her attention to the breathing process. Even though the person is concentrate on the breathing, he/she will notice how the mind wanders off. This passive observation should be made without any judgment; the practice of meditation is an important part of the mindfulness practice, allowing people to escape the judgments they often place upon their own thoughts, feelings and sensations.

The meditation process is not lengthy and most of the practitioners prefer short sessions, which last somewhere around ten minutes. The important thing is that the sessions are practiced regularly; the more you practice, the easier it will become for you to stay concentrated on the breathing process. The practice of mindfulness is strongly connected to the one of breathing; one of its objectives is for the practitioner to become more aware of his/her breathing. This leads in time to mindful awareness, allowing the person to focus on the present thoughts, feelings and sensations.

How can mindfulness meditation help? There are multiple answers to this question, starting with the fact that such practices are known to reduce the negative effects of psychological stress. Meditation is recommended, along with mindfulness exercises, in people who experience chronic pain, as it is known to reduce the severity of that pain. Also, once introduced in patients diagnosed with anxiety disorder, depression or chronic stress, it has shown significant improvements whereas the symptoms presented were concerned.

The Buddhist practice remains at the root of mindfulness and meditation. The meditation process, based on these ancient practices, leads to an increase state of awareness of the present self. In turn, the raised awareness will help a person become calmer and handle his/her emotions more effectively. Whether a person suffers from anxiety, depression or chronic psychological stress, that person will soon discover the psychological and cognitive improvements that meditation has brought in a short period of time.

As a beginner into the world of mindfulness and meditation, you have two possibilities. You can either learn the meditation techniques by yourself or you can join a group, learning these techniques in a formal setting. The good news is that you have complete liberty when it comes to taking such decisions. Plus, one you start to practice meditation, it will become a natural habit and you will soon be able to enter in the state of meditation without too much effort. Regardless of the problems you had in the past, you will discover that your quality of life has improved to a level you never expected.

The biggest benefit that mindfulness meditation will bring to you is related to the stress in your life. The more you practice meditation, the better you will be able to handle any stressful situation. You will feel calm and enjoy the recent peace of mind, feeling like you have a clear image of your future. Overall, you will find balance in your life, enjoying the physical and psychological well-being.

Chapter 3: Breathing Techniques

Effective use of breathing techniques can help you in several ways. Possibly most important, they allow you to concentrate on something that is not going to impinge your meditative process. It is only natural that we tend to get distracted easily because that's how the thought patterns in our minds have developed. These distractions might be singular, random thoughts, or more like a chain of thoughts, and this is often due to the reason that there is nothing else engaging enough (that also does not prompt avoidance) to occupy our mind at the time. Thus, when you learn to practice the breathing techniques mentioned later in this chapter, you will find there are multiple benefits, such as:

Allows you to slow down the thought process

Lower blood pressure and heart rate to align with a resting rate

Lower levels of cortisol (i.e., a stress-inducing hormone) and reduce the harmful effects associated with high levels

Prompts release of endorphins (i.e., a stress-reducing hormone)

Prompts function of the lymphatic system to release harmful toxins

Improves oxygen delivery to the heart, additional to all cells, which goes on to improve every system of the body

Allows muscle relaxation and physical tension release

While achieving mindfulness as a whole can be quite daunting, practicing basic breathing techniques is an easily achievable first step that enables you to become more aware of your breathing and, in turn, more aware of the silence required in mind to benefit from mindful practice. You may not yet be ready to progress to a state of meditation. However, there's no reason to avoid practicing basic breathing techniques to begin your journey in the right direction.

Positioning

Positioning yourself with good posture is key to maintaining and practicing effective breathing techniques, and you always need to be in a position where your back is straight. The Hindus believe that the spine should be straight because of an individual's energy flow, and they also describe the areas down your spine as 'chakras' (focal points of the subtle body used in meditation practices). If you slouch, the energy is unable to pass through your body. Whether you are approaching breathing techniques in a traditional meditative context, or simply in the hope to improve your health and mood, a straight back with good posture and shoulders set slightly back to open the chest is vital before you commence breathing practice.

Breathing

Once your posture and body are ready, let's dive into a breathing technique. Keep your head straight and close your eyes to minimize distraction. Breathe in through your nostrils while counting to nine. While it may seem difficult to reach nine on one breath, the idea of this exercise is not that you keep counting, but to determine the length of breath needed and eventually fall into a natural pattern of breathing longer breaths without the need to count. Slowly release through an outward breath that should last a little longer – you are expelling excess oxygen from your system and drawing breath from deep down in your diaphragm, so you feel a pivoting motion as you breathe, and thus a slightly longer duration is needed. Again, draw another breath in to the count of nine and slowly exhale to the count of eleven. Visualization can be a great help in this exercise by perceiving a breath to take on a physical form, such as visualizing oneself inhaling flames of a fire and exhaling a controlled icy breeze. Use of visualization can also really help to ground the individual at the moment. Again, practice inhaling the flickering flames to the count of nine, then slowly exhale a cold, controlled wind.

But what if thoughts enter my mind and distract me from the task at hand? Simple. Simply acknowledge the thought and let it go again. For example, imagine you enter a room full of people. For that moment you enter, their thoughts are focused on you, and they acknowledge your entrance. As quickly as you are acknowledged by the crowd for entering, the acknowledgement soon ceases, and they return to their conversations and movements that occurred prior to your entry. Your thought processes should follow a similar pattern. Of course, there will always be thoughts you need to deal with and turn your attention to for longer periods throughout your life, but to practice breathing techniques, try to focus only on the motion of breathing and return yourself to be in the moment should your mind wander. When you finish your breathing exercise, please remember not to get up too quickly. If you've practiced deep breathing successfully, it is more than likely your blood pressure has lowered in the process, and thus we don't want to end a session with any injuries! Instead, take a moment to reflect and re-engage with your surroundings as you prepare to return to your day.

The beauty of practicing breathing techniques is you can perform them at any time, and often anywhere. Sitting on a park bench at lunchtime, you can simply breathe and allow the fresh air to fill your lungs to refresh you in the day. Regularly practicing deep breathing will enable you to feel calmer and is great practice for meditation. Your environment is particularly important when practicing breathing techniques as you often absorb your environment's ambience and, as Western culture says, "smell the roses". You are present in the moment, and deep breathing will allow all of your senses to come alive and coordinate with one another. The scents you can smell, the items you can touch, the sights you can see and the things you can hear all compose that moment into being. Particularly if you are in a public environment, try to embrace every of your sense's responses as this is key to truly embracing the moment.

As I mentioned earlier, the concept of mindfulness as a whole can sometimes be too daunting and making a bold decision such as "I want to be a mindful person", or "I want to practice mindfulness" can entail too much initially to effectively begin. Mindfulness is a series of processes that contribute to a greater picture, so starting with smaller steps such as learning breathing techniques or practicing control and acceptance of your thought patterns can be far more rewarding and encourage you to delve deeper into your journey on a mindful path.

Chapter 4: The Psychological Benefits Of Meditation

Stress

It's fair to say that stress is an epidemic in the modern world. Meditation has been shown to have a significant effect on reducing stress. It helps us focus on being present, taking us to a state of deep relaxation. It stimulates the chemicals within our brain responsible for feeling happy and energized. It also reduces the physical size the parts of our brain that are responsible for making us feel anxious and fearful.

Neurogenesis

Just prior to birth, humans have around a trillion neurons in their brains. Unfortunately, by adulthood, that number is closer to 100 billion, a significant drop. As you age, the number continues to decrease. This is normal and was believed to be irreversible. However, a study published in the journal of Nature Medicine in 1998 changed this thinking. It was found that the brain is able to regenerate neurons. Just like someone who does nothing to keep themselves healthy and fit finds their body becoming fat, weak and sick, the brain is the same. In order to keep it fit, strong and healthy, it needs to be exercised. Learning a language, creating art, doing mind puzzles and so on can all help generate healthy new neurons, but by far the champion as generating fresh new neurons is meditation.

Meditation not only balances both hemispheres of your brain, but it actually makes it stronger, healthier and helps it rewire itself in a way that allows your ability for higher thinking to be dramatically improved.

All of this can have a profound effect on the psychological aspects of how your brain functions. It improves memory, IQ, attention span and thought processing while reducing activity associated with fear, anxiety, depression and anger.

With continued meditation, your entire nervous system is soon rewired, organizing itself to the optimum level throughout your body.

Disorders of the Mind

Addiction. Do you have any bad habits? Do you bite your nails, smoke, or drink too much, or have an addiction to prescribed or illegal drugs? These are all indicators of something not being quite right with the way your brain is functioning.

Meditation can help you to understand the reasons behind your behavior and stop justifying reasons not to change. It will help you see the benefits of your life if those behaviors didn't control you.

A study on heavy social drinkers showed that meditation and other structured relaxation techniques resulted in a significant reduction of their alcohol intake.

Similar studies with smoking and drug taking have shown the same kind of results. In one study, prisoners who were addicted to drugs were given an intensive course of meditation over a 12-week period. They meditated for 30 minutes twice a day. The results of this not only improved the prisoners overall mental state but also allowed them to give up their drug habits better than any other rehabilitation program that had been tried.

Phobias. Often when people are afraid of something they say they have a phobia. The truth is that a real phobia is a serious and complex psychological disorder. It not only has a negative effect on the person's everyday life but can cause them to have irrational responses and even dangerous responses. All panic disorders are driven by the fight or flight instinct within the primitive subconscious part of our brain. Using meditation actually shrinks and breaks many of the connections to this part of our brain, which alleviates our fear response and can over time help phobia sufferers recover.

Obsessive-Compulsive Disorder (OCD). For someone suffering from OCD, the continual intrusive thoughts that cause them to act in a way that to others seems irrational or excessive to non-sufferers is a daily challenge. From stressing about the germs on the handle of the shopping cart to obsessing over avoiding the cracks in the pavements it can take many forms and become an endless barrage of thoughts that rob the sufferer from freedom.

Our brains have, for the average person, in the region of 70,000 thoughts a day. For someone suffering with OCD, this number can be far greater. The number put forward by the American Psychological Association was "Too many."

This is a result of the conscious mind being overloaded and happens also in anxiety and depression.

Meditation allows you greater access to your subconscious mind. It stops compulsive behavior and allows your mind to refocus on other things. It promotes creativity and better sleep while reducing stress, anxiety and depression.

Eating Disorders. Eating disorders can be exceedingly difficult to overcome. But meditation has been seen to provide great benefits. It can help sufferers to focus thoughts on more productive things, release tension aiding relaxation, promote a feeling of self-confidence and decrease the urges. It helps you to learn that a happy, healthy life is attainable. Most importantly it teaches you how to love you for who you are. This is achieved primarily from changes to chemical balance in the brain.

Other psychological illnesses also benefit from the regular practice of meditation including Depression, Dementia, Alzheimer's, ADHD and ADD and Bipolar Disorder.

Chapter 5: Observing Your Thoughts

Our mind is the most complex matter in the world, and even scientists are shocked at the complexity in our minds these days. So our mind was supposed to serve us and not burden us with unproductive thoughts. We seem to be able to let our emotions rule our lives to the point of devastation that can cause both physical and mental health issues.

If you're one who likes to let your emotions control the way you're behaving and thinking, then I have a few tips that can help. In reality, thoughts are not at all bad, they can cause in our bodies a natural drug that acts as an anti-depressant that makes us feel good and comfortable. These are positive thoughts, but it is the negative thinking that can cause a whole new set of emotions like fear, stress, frustration, etc. By analyzing each thought as it moves through our heads, we can take back control of the way we think, similar to understanding what an advantage and a liability is. When you know that a certain thought is an advantage to hang on to that thought as long as you can to pull all the positive energy from it, and if you sense a negative thought coming into your mind then catch it, now when I say grab it, you need to stop it right in its tracks before it causes an emotional reaction and throw it away.

Or you can sit back and watch your thoughts from a distance as they go in and out of your mind, you're just watching your thoughts from a positive or negative setting, it's important you don't add any emotional response to those thoughts you're just watching. The purpose of this exercise is to see how much is going through your mind that will give less control and power over you to those negative thoughts. The main thing is that before they reach that emotional stage, you take as much of the positive energy from good thoughts and stop those negative thoughts in their tracks.

If you want to do more than visit Thought Control and kill those unwanted thoughts once and for all, there are yet more methods that you can use to conquer negative thoughts.

Did you know you can study yourself? One characteristic that separates us, humans, from animals is the capacity to self-observe. Sadly, it is quite clear that not much attention is paid to this profound capacity in today's world.

This self-observing-self is quickly put into words, but I found (based on my own experience and the experience of some of my friends trying it out) that it wasn't that easy to do. What is that meaning? How can the self be a self-observer?

It can, no doubt about it - and there's nothing new about it. Freud called it something like "the interested and unmoving observer/witness. "A well-known contemporary figure, it was beautifully characterized by Eckhart Tolle as" looking at the thinker. I heard about' metadata' that is data regarding data when I studied computer sciences, and I used to equate it with' meta thinking'- thinking about thinking.

This is very pragmatic; you don't have to believe me when I say it can be done just do it on your own. Personally, listening to Tolle's explanation was a huge eye-opener for me, and that helped a lot.

If you've never done it, try it, look at your reflections.

Okay, now you might ask, "Well, how do I look at my thoughts?" That's also what happened to me. I used to be perplexed about what my reflections might look like. Finally, what I did was to imagine "taking my mind back into observation mode and watching my thoughts like watching a film."

Thoughts come in the images as well as in the inner voices. For example, we may see a broken-hearted man in silence in a film, but we also hear a voice (his voice) saying, "She no longer loves me." Bingo, that's the sound inside. I'm sure you've heard those voices before in your head, but we never know you're listening. And that's a big element-consciousness. You're now' conscious' that you can watch, you can watch whenever you like.

Control of Your Life with Mindfulness

It is very difficult to cope with the world's fast pace and many stressful situations have to be handled by people most of the time. Meditation is one of the easiest ways to cope with stress in order to lead a hale and heart-felt life. There are many forms of meditation techniques involved. Meditation of mindfulness is one of them. This is not a difficult technique at all.

By following some simple steps, one can easily practice this. This CD is available on the market easily. You will learn the right methods and practice them without any hassles with the aid of the CD. This is a very old meditation technique that has been practiced for a very long time. It is said that Gautama Buddha is teaching it. The main object a person has to concentrate on can be his breath in it. When a person learns how to observe breathing, a quiet and peaceful state of mind will be experienced. With the aid of it, one can achieve inner peace. The steps were also very easy to eat. This mainly involves sitting upright and focusing on breathing. There's no need to manipulate the mind's coming thoughts. Every thought that comes to his mind, a person should embrace.

If you are just a novice, there's no need to practice intensive meditation techniques. There are simple steps, to begin with for beginners. Guided Mindfulness Meditation is a kind of technique of meditation that beginners can easily practice. You just need to learn the basic steps to practice Guided Mindfulness Meditation. In Guided meditation of mindfulness, one must learn to experience life and whatever it brings into the path of life. Guided meditation of mindfulness helps you improve your relationship with your worries, issues, tension and pains. Meditation does not encourage us to neglect or run away from your problems, rather it helps us to be more open about them. Use guided meditation, one can gain wisdom to accept and address all the experiences life gives you.

Chapter 6: Mindfulness: The Art Of Cultivating Resilience

Undeniably, sooner or latter, we all have to deal with life's realities-those hard surprises and "unknowns" that can literally change everything in less than a nanosecond.

Imagine you've just been fired. Many of us would react to this situation in at least some of the following ways:

"I'm terrified."

"I should have seen this coming."

"I'll never find another job in this economy."

"Am I going to be homeless?"

"I'm a failure."

Reactions like these reflect a fear-based survival framework for viewing the situation, whereby we filter the external facts of what's happening through the internal lens of what we feel (our thoughts, feelings, beliefs and body sensations). In this way, our fear creates our reality, locking us in anger, powerlessness, and blame.

Mindfulness: A Tool for Re-contextualizing and Reframing

"People are not afraid of things, but of how they view them."- Epictetus

Although it's understandable why we might react from fear when facing the prospect of losing our job, or other challenging situations, Mindfulness is a powerful tool that offers us the opportunity to make a radical shift in orientation.

Mindfulness is the practice of bringing our awareness to what we are experiencing in the present, both internally and externally, without judgment (Kornfield, 2009). It is a wake-up call to become conscious of the ways we perceive and respond to life's situations. When we live mindfully, we shift our entire ground of being.

Here's a traditional, easy-to-follow exercise to help develop your mindfulness during difficult situations (Klau, 2009). Mindfulness takes time to develop. It is an ongoing process. Be kind and compassionate to yourself as you follow these instructions.

1) Sit in a quiet room where you won't be disturbed.
2) Close your eyes and focus your attention on your breath.
3) It's natural for your attention to become distracted. When that happens, simply return to your breath.
4) While focusing on your breath, allow your thoughts, feelings, beliefs, and body sensations to enter your awareness as you perceive the external situation.
5) Now ask yourself: What are the facts of the situation? What are my thoughts, feelings, beliefs and body sensations? How am I responding?

With practice, this exercise can bring us to our calm, reflective center. This safe-haven, in which we can rest and see more clearly, holds and contains everything arising for us in the present. From here, it is possible to deconstruct, re-contextualize and reframe our original fear-based feelings and reactions, honoring and embracing them without being their victims.1

For example, let's return to the original situation, where you've just lost your job. Rather than automatically reacting with fear, Mindfulness helps you realize and accept: "The only fact about this situation is that I don't have my job right now. Everything else- my self-judgment, my fear, my blame, my anger, and the tightness in my body- is my feelings."

We don't have to meditate to practice being mindful. There are many ways to incorporate mindfulness into our daily lives. As we become increasingly mindful, we can begin to respond from a place of freedom and choice.

In other words, we can act with resilience.

What Does Resilient Living Look Like?

The more mindful we become, we broaden and build several inner resources that help us strengthen our resilience (Fredrickson, 2001). These include:

• Compassion: You hold the intention not to judge yourself or others. You are mindful of your self-talk. However, if you do judge yourself, you don't judge yourself for judging. You are kinder and more supportive. If mindfulness brings the wisdom to see clearly, then compassion brings a loving heart (Neff, 2011).

• Acceptance: You increasingly accept the facts, which you can distinguish from the feelings. Acceptance isn't about "giving up." It is having the strength to "let go" of control and stop fighting reality.

• Openness: You're progressively open to viewing even the most difficult situations as opportunities for growth. You trust that they have something to teach you, and you expect to learn.

• Creativity: You draw on your power to visualize and create the results you desire.

At the same time, in the spirit of acceptance, you are not attached or fixated upon your own expectations.

Living resiliently is more than just "bouncing back." It is about shifting our perceptions, changing our responses, and learning something new. For example, a resilient response to losing our job might re-contextualize and reframe the situation in any of the following ways:

"I'm going to breathe deeply and take things one step at a time."

"I may not like it, but this is the way it is. My first step will be to file for unemployment."

"I'm not going to play 'the blame game.' It's not my boss' fault or mine."

"I'm sure that there's a lesson or two for me to learn from all this."

"It would be easy to get 'just another job.' I'm going to find one that I'm truly passionate about."

In Conclusion

Living resiliently represents a whole new way of being and doing.

In this way, resilience isn't just for the hard times- it's for all times. Empowering us to live, love, and work adventurously in the face of change, it builds a well from which we can draw for the rest of our lives.

Chapter 7: Mind Maintenance

Once you have freed your mind from the noise that tends to build up there, it is important to maintain it. Think of your brain as you would your muscles. You don't just build them and keep them, you need to continuously work to maintain them.

There are lots of little ways to maintain a clutter-free mind. The first thing is to avoid accumulating more clutter. Just as you would eliminate physical things that pile up in your home, you need to keep tabs on how you are feeling mentally, physically and spiritual at all times to avoid ending up right back where you started.

Remember that feeling tired despite good sleep habits is an early sign that your mind is cluttered. You are likely not sleeping as well as you think, and what brainpower you do have during the day is preoccupied with thoughts that don't serve you.

Do yourself a favor and take some time to check in with your thoughts every day. Are you feeling energized and clear? Is your brain foggy and sluggish? Do you feel anxious, angry or sad? Assess where you are so you can spend some time making improvements when necessary.

A great way to get in touch with your inner spirit and check in with your thoughts is to meditate. Taking just ten or fifteen minutes every day to sit and be inside your mind is a great practice. Meditation can be very simple and doesn't need to cut into your day. Set your alarm clock a few minutes early and take that time to lay in bed and simply think. If you feel you might fall asleep, physically sit up in bed, or try at another time of day.

Focus on the sound of your breath, or invest in a guided meditation soundtrack. The goal is to quickly get in touch with your inner self so that it can guide you. We all have an inner voice that helps us plan our day and our lives, but very few of us actually listen.

Some people say that exercise is a form of meditation, and to each their own. It is scientifically proven that exercise of all types helps reduce stress hormones, calm nerves and promote emotional well-being. Of course, it also strengthens the body and immune system as well, leading to better overall health.

Something as simple as taking a walk outside every day is enough to help clear your mind and get you thinking optimally again. If you tend to get inside your head when you are exercising, try using the activity as a dual meditation session. That is, concentrate and focus only on what you are doing. If you are out walking in the woods, take in the scenery and try to let other thoughts float to the back burner.

No matter the activity, it is important to give your mind time to rest and recover. Your brain is a sensitive organ, just like any other. It needs downtime to restore proper function. We can see the truth in this by recognizing how sluggish and foggy we are when we are running on little sleep. Downtime while awake is just as vital. Think of this downtime as an opportunity for the tiny librarians in your brain to sort through all of the open books and put them back on the shelves. Having this time to gather your thoughts makes you better able to make sense of them later.

People who are overworked often slip into their performance because they work TOO much. Yes, there is such a thing, despite what some of the world's most eccentric billionaires tell you. Taking breaks and allowing for rest actually makes you a better worker, allows you to be more alert and active in your daily life, and more proactive for your future.

On that note, keeping the past in the past and the future in the future is also vital to preventing the buildup of mental clutter. The most important moment in life is the one you are living right now. The rest is history, and we cannot predict what will happen in the future. There is no sense in worrying about things we do not yet know, and worrying means you are only suffering a second time provided that it actually comes to fruition.

Instead, take a mindful stance, and concentrate on being present and active at the moment. Focus on the work that you are doing, appreciate that you are hanging out with family and friends, and do things that strike your fancy at the moment. Learn to appreciate the subtle intricacies that are life, and soak in every moment. You truly don't know when your time is up. Do you really want to go out thinking about that horrible meeting you had yesterday?

A good rule of thumb is to check in with yourself at least three times during the day. Ask yourself a few good questions: Do you remember the ins and outs of what you have done over the past few hours? Do you feel as if you have accomplished something? Do you feel content? Excited? Agitated? Truly take stock of that time and decide where to fit in some balance. If you worked hard the last few hours, maybe it's time to give your brain a quick break and do something fun and silly for a few minutes.

What can you do in the next few hours to improve yourself? Find a shred of happiness and joy? Something that will propel you into the future you have always dreamed of? You must always keep thoughts of your innermost desires close to the front of your brain. Think of them as your operating manual. Are you acting in such a way that is in line with your innermost needs and morals? What can you do to better live those dreams?

Remember that mental clutter will dissipate more and more as you get closer to living your true inner passions and dreams. The energy of the universe will flow in your favor if you just give in to what your inner self truly desires. It's what YOU want, so why are you fighting it?

Chapter 8: Mindfulness Meditation

There are numerous ways that you can practice mindfulness, which is not limited to just meditation. Different forms of yoga, tai chi, Qi Chong and other ancient practices, actually incorporate the practice of mindfulness, but in a more physical or dynamic way.

The whole point of mindfulness is just about become more present and learning to be more aware of everything that is around you (and any internal dialogue as well) occurring in the here and now. We will be focusing on the how to practice mindfulness meditation in this book, as it is essentially very simple and you don't need any equipment or experienced guide. Find a quiet place where you can sit comfortably. You can sit any way that feels comfortable; crossed legged or even on a chair, whatever you prefer. Close your eyes and sit with your back straight and in a comfortable posture.

Now focus on your breathing. Feel the rise and fall of your chest and try to gently make your breathing become more and more calm. Maybe even start breathing deeper, so that your breath goes down into your belly. This will bring a greater sense of calm because you are breathing deeper, as opposed to just breathing normally where your chest expands and contracts. Repeat these breathing steps.

Now when you feel a little bit calmer, it's time to shift your awareness to your surroundings. With eyes still closed, try and focus on what you can hear, the distinct and small sounds all around you. Then focus on your other senses. Can you feel the ground that you are sitting on? Is there a certain scent within the air? Be mindful of all your other senses (while keeping your eyes closed of course).

What you will most likely find is that your mind will repeatedly wander, usually to worrisome thoughts about the past or future. Thoughts occur so effortlessly. This is the nature of the mind. We are always envisioning our future, or reminiscing on the past. If your mind wanders, simply bring your awareness back to your breath.

Consistency is key so try to make it a habit to practice this technique every day. There is no set time that you need to meditate for. Always go for quality rather than quantity. If you're sitting and closing your eyes, but you do not practice the techniques of breathing correctly and focusing your awareness, then you're not going to get the full benefits of mindfulness training. Maybe try mindfulness meditation for 2 minutes at the start or for a set number of breaths and then slowly work your way up over time.

Mindfulness meditation requires yielding

Mindfulness practice is all about being present and experiencing the present moment, while letting go of ego or judgement. This requires yielding to the thoughts which enter your mind.

Whatever thought passes through your mind, do not judge it, simply acknowledge it and then focus on breathing deeper and calmer. The more you try to force or will your way to stop the thoughts you have, the harder it will be to stop the reoccurring thoughts. You shouldn't try to will your way or try 'harder', there's an element of letting go or yielding. You will find all sorts of crazy thoughts entering your mind, but you need to learn to yield to them and let them go.

Whatever method you try for your mindfulness practice, it is important to realise that consistency is key. You really need to make it a habit to practice mindfulness every day, in order to really benefit from this practice. Maybe wake up 10 minutes earlier than you're use to and practicing mindfulness meditation, before your day begins. Slowly but surely, you will become more efficient and effective at mindfulness practice, and its benefits will show up in your daily life.

Chapter 9: Body Awareness/Scan

Mindfulness

The reality of life without mindfulness is that it is full of never-ending confusion and disagreement between your body and your mind. Your mind is never where your body is. While engaged in one activity, your mind will be busy thinking about the things you failed to do, all the missteps of the past, or worrying about what to do and the right steps to take in the future. This affects your peace of mind, job productivity, relationship, health, and every other important aspect of your life.

Without the awareness mindfulness brings, you can be with your spouse or kids and still not be present. You can be with them and lost in thoughts about your new projects, uncertainties about your job, bills to pay, and all other such life's worries. Awareness helps bring your mind home from its unending journeys.

By now, you have generated enough mindfulness energy through your deep breathing exercises and can now channel that energy towards recognizing the language your body speaks and all of its realities and desires.

Awareness of your body helps align your mind and body so they can work in harmony. This alignment and agreement between your mind and body helps you live in the present moment and enjoy the beautiful moments of your everyday life as life happens. This reality fills you with joy and helps you become in touch with the true wonders and miracle of being alive within and around you.

How to Practice Body Awareness Mindfulness

Here are the steps that will help you foster increased body awareness:

Begin with deep breathing, and while you draw in breaths, tell yourself, "I'm aware of my body." This will bring your focus to your body.

Begin from any part of your body and become aware of how that body part feels at that moment. You can begin from feet and work your way up to the crown of your head.

Think about each body part and all it helps you accomplish. The best way to understand how important every body part is to your life is to imagine life without it. Imagine life without your legs. As you imagine this, you will experience a surge of appreciation for all the places your legs help you go and all you can accomplish daily and in your life because you have legs and can walk.

Do this with every other part of your body and become aware of what each part is saying or needs. You can notice pains and as you become more aware, give each body part the care and attention it needs to serve you better.

Upon ending your mindfulness session—this and all the others—translate the awareness to your daily living by taking advanced steps to improve your awareness.

Place yourself under intense observation under different situations to know where and when you function better. This will help you become more aware of your strengths and weaknesses.

Keep a journal and write down all the emotions, feelings, and sensations that accompany each experience. Go through this journal daily so you can become more aware of your personality, strengths, and weaknesses to make important adjustments.

Get feedback from people around you. Ask people around you what they think about you and the things they think you can change to become better. This will help you become more self-aware.

Chapter 10: Muscle Relaxation

We have already discussed the importance of relaxing the body before meditation. This chapter will delve deeper specifically into muscle relaxation exercises, which you can do as a stand-alone session to relax your body or use before meditation to ensure your body is completely relaxed.

This exercise should never be painful. If you feel pain at any time, you should stop. Try again—but more gently this time. If pain persists, this might mean that there is something amiss. Check with your doctor to make sure there is nothing wrong.

This form of muscle relaxation is to tense a particular muscle or muscle group—hold that tension, and then relax. This will achieve two things: the act of tensing a muscle and holding it will force it to relax when you finally let go, and you will learn over time just what a relaxed muscle feels like, making it easier for you to relax your muscles at will as you continue to practice this exercise.

Begin with having a proper poster. Refer to the section above if you need to refresh yourself. Now, concentrate on your breathing so you can focus on your muscles. Again, refer to the breathing exercises above if you need. Now, you have yourself ready physically, begin to tense and release your muscles one by one. Try to keep breathing slowly and controlled while you focus.

Move from your lower extremities upward. Start with the muscles in your legs. Tense them and hold. Examine how they feel. Try to tense them further. Feel how the muscles want to let go, but don't just yet. Tense even more, until you feel you can't tighten any further. Hold this state and count slowly to five. Now, relax your muscles. Feel them let go, how the tension disappears and your legs seem to go limp. Study how this feels. This is your leg muscles truly relaxed.

Now, do the same for your arms. From your shoulders to your hands, tighten everything you can. Ball your hands into fists. Feel the tension. Now, squeeze your muscles harder. Then harder yet. When you feel you can't tighten them any further, once again, count slowly to five and then relax. Now, feel the tension in your arms fall way, feel the muscles go limp and truly relax. Study this feeling in your arms. This is how they feel when they are relaxed.

Now, concentrate on your bottom. Tighten your gluteal muscles. Hold the tension. Tense them again. Hold again. Now, tighten them until you feel you can't hold any longer. Again, count slowly to five, then relax. Just like with your arms and legs, take note of how your gluteal muscles feel when relaxed.

Concentrate on your back now. While maintaining your breathing, tense the muscles in your back. Hold and then tense some more. As above, tighten until you feel you're at your limit, count to five, and relax. But maintain your posture.

Notice how your back muscles feel when relaxed.

Turn now to your front. Tighten the muscles in your stomach and chest. Use the three-step process outlined above. Examine the tension, then increase it. Finally, increase until you feel you must let go, count to five, and relax. Pay attention to how the muscles in your trunk feel now.

Finally, turn your attention to your face. Tighten all the muscles you can (there are 43 in total). Clamp your eyes shut, wrinkle your nose. Don't worry about making a funny face. That's the idea. Again, examine how this feels, then continue to increase the tension until you reach your limit. Count to five, and let go. Now, pay attention to the muscles in your face. This is how they feel when relaxed.

Now, take stock of your body. Examine how your muscles feel. If any pockets of tension remain, allow them to drift away.

Your body is now relaxed. Notice your breathing, pay attention to it. Appreciate you relaxed breathing. Appreciate your relaxed body. Take some time to enjoy it.

If this is a warm up to a meditation session, you should begin now. If you were only looking to relax, you can now begin to come out of the exercise. Start by moving your fingers and toes, then slowly return to your regular state. You should spend a few minutes simply walking, perhaps gently shaking out your legs, and gently swinging your arms.

After this exercise, you should feel calm and refreshed.

Chapter Summary. Pay attention to these items in order to successfully relax your muscles.

Posture

Breathing

Start with the legs, then arms, back, front, and face.

Take a few moments to enjoy the sensation when you have completed the exercise.

Chapter 11: Thinking

First things first. We've already laid out some general rules but this chapter will provide you with the framework for structuring your practice. In order to become proficient with the technique, we need to lay down some groundwork. It won't take long and there is very little to remember, but some practice is needed in the beginning to get the knack.

The first thing I'm going to teach you is based on the mediation technique called "noting." The basic idea is that you note every sensation and thought that enters your field of experience. This sounds difficult because a lot of the time we deal with concepts. In this practice, we're only going to deal with pure, ground-level body sensations and thoughts.

We make a few distinctions and assumptions for the sake of the practice. They might not necessarily be true, so just take them as the scaffolding for which we'll hang our meditation experience. This is not about believing anything new, just doing the training as it works best.

The first thing to talk about is experience. For the sake of the training, let's just assume that any experience you have can be broken into 2 separate categories – body and mind. You can only ever experience something through your 5 senses – which I would call sensory experience or body. There is a 6th experience you can have that we will consider your 6th sense – thinking. When we use the term 6th sense here, we're not referring to ESP or anything esoteric, just every day thinking. So any experience you have is either body, mind or body + mind in as many combinations as you can find by adding together the 6 senses.

Let's look at anger for a minute. Typically, the experience of anger is a combination of body sensations and thoughts. It often starts as a thought, then you can feel something in your chest, maybe a rising pressure or heat, then that causes more thoughts to boil up which in turn cause more feelings of anger in the body and while it's all happening, you use one word to call the entire combination of experiences "anger."

For now, let's just deal with the body sensations and thoughts.

A lot of what we're going to talk about has been inspired by the work of Shinzen Young. He has done an amazing job of quantifying experience in mediation and uses very specific language during practice. We'll be using a simplified version of his system in addition to some other techniques.

So here is what you need to know about using words to "note" your experience. Try this right now, just look at something in the room you're in. While you're looking at the thing (or things) just mentally repeat in your head, "seeing, seeing, seeing."

The voice in your head shouldn't be shouting, but rather a soft voice and should only take up about 5 -10% of your mental power. The rest of your attention should be on the thing you're seeing.

Do this now, look at something and mentally repeat, "seeing, seeing, seeing." You can do it slowly for now; the trick is to leave no gap between the mental rep of the word "seeing" because that is when your wandering mind will try to sneak in.

There – you've now practiced the art of noting. Seeing is probably the easiest of the senses to use but we'll get into all of them.

The beauty of this method and why I chose this above all other meditation methods to teach beginners is the act of mental noting does something very important. It serves to block out stray thinking and daydreaming. One of the common complaints of beginning meditators is they tend to drift off into random thinking and daydreaming after only meditating for a few minutes. When you're actively noting, you prevent most, but not all, stray thought. The more you practice, the less wandering thought will creep in.

I spent years "trying" to meditate but unable to get anywhere because my imagination would kick in. Or I would start thinking about stuff I had to do later that day. Noting blocks a lot of the mental noise you normally experience.

One of the great benefits of this form of meditation is that it forces you to focus on one thing at a time. So you get a much-needed break from the exhaustion of constant compulsive thought. To be able to silence the mind on-demand is a great skill to have and gives the mind a much needed break.

So what happens when you do happen to fall into stray thought? You probably already guessed it, you note it "thinking, thinking, thinking." Obviously, you won't be able to do this while you're thinking the thought, but you can do it as soon as you catch yourself, right after thinking the thought. While you're noting "thinking, thinking, thinking" you stop the flood of thought that leads to more thought. It's like plugging a leak.

Don't think or expect to have a meditation session right away where you don't fall into thought. The great part is now you can turn it into part of your mindfulness practice. You catch yourself, focus on the thought, note it and then go back to your object of concentration. We will specifically discuss your object of concentration in just a bit.

The fact that you're noting makes it a lot easier to notice when you fall into thought and aren't noting. Little by little, you'll start to build your concentration muscle by pointing your attention on certain things (like seeing) and noting those things. You will get better at concentrating. This ability is related to success in all aspects of life. If you can't concentrate on something, you won't be able to learn or deal with the subject skillfully.

For the purpose of this book, we'll deal with the following senses:

Seeing – Refers to the act of seeing. We just want to be aware of what we're seeing. So we never note the label of the actual thing we're seeing (like "wall"). Always focus on the seeing. So for instance, you may be staring at a point on the wall saying "seeing, seeing, seeing." You would never say "wall, wall, wall." I'll talk more about this later, but we want to concentrate on our experience of seeing. This is very important.

Touching – This is another strong sensation we can use in our meditation. Touching in this sense refers to our external touch. As I'm writing this, I'm aware of my butt on the seat of the chair where I'm sitting. So I would note that as "touching, touching, touching" and focus on the sensations that I'm aware of. I just rested for a minute with my hands on the keyboard. Again, that's "touching, touching, touching" and I'm focusing on the sensations I'm noticing through my fingers on the laptop.

Feeling – We use the term "feeling" to note any internal body sensations we feel. We may feel happiness or anger or boredom. Those words are often referring to sensations inside our body that combined with the label of thought begin to form the experience we call emotions. We want to avoid noting an emotion, but rather look at the sensations inside the body that make up that experience. Instead of noting "excitement, you are better off noting and looking at the tenseness, relaxation, tingling and other sensations that make up the feeling of excitement. A lot of times people talk of body sensations break-up into vibrations. These are just body sensations chunked down into smaller components. It may take a little bit of time to get to this point, but you will come to enjoy the subtle massage of these vibrating and moving body sensations.

Hearing – Many meditation practices use hearing as the object of concentration. If you really look at it, it has a strange quality. You can hear a truck outside, but the hearing itself happens at the ear. For many traditions, looking into this specific quality can open up many lines of inquiry into the nature of experience. You are certainly free to experiment with it that way, but in the beginning I recommend using it in a different way. When you're meditating, it is often difficult to find a spot that is completely free from noise. I don't think I've ever meditated, even in meditation halls with monks that had no external noise. Even just sitting there you will hear the noise of your own breathing. In this book, we'll be mostly focusing on using the breath as your object of concentration. While you're focusing on the breath (don't worry, I'll give you precise instructions how to do that using the noting technique in just a bit) you may get pulled away by the sound of birds outside. Or a truck lumbering down the road. Or a siren in the distance. Simply put your awareness on the sound and note it "hearing, hearing, hearing." Just like with thought, you will burn away the distraction. If it's a noise that disappears after just a few seconds, like a bird chirping, then note it and go back to the breath. If it's a constant noise, you may want to note it for a little while longer before going back to the breath. You'll find that noting a sound takes away a bit of the pull of that sound. In the process of putting your awareness on the distraction, you're also practicing momentary concentration. This is great, because any distraction becomes just more fuel for your practice.

Thinking – We talked a bit about this already. When you're noting, you use the "thinking, thinking, thinking" label a lot like the "hearing, hearing, hearing" label. It acts as a way to ward off distractions in the form of thoughts. Thoughts only come in two forms. They're either in the form of Talk or Image (both mental). If you can notice what kind of thought you're having, you can label it Talk (self-talk inside your head) or Image (a picture you make with your mind). There is literally no other kind of thought you can have. See, thinking isn't that big of a deal when you break it down. It is also good practice to use this technique off the cushion so to speak. If you are having a negative thought before giving a presentation, just become aware of it and note "thinking, thinking, thinking" – the amazing thing is that after just a little bit of noting, it usually goes away. And whereas in the past it may have sucked you in and spiraled off into more negative self-talk, with this technique it usually just goes away. It's almost like a little child that wants attention. Once you give it attention, it goes off on its way. Sure, it might come back, especially in the early days of your practice. But once you have some proficiency, usually just noting an experience for a little bit is enough to make it disappear. This works with unpleasant body sensations too – but the more overwhelming the sensation, the more attention and noting you may need to place on it.

The above list of 5 things is all you need to get started with one of the most powerful meditation techniques on the planet. Please note, we left taste and smell off the list. For our purposes and to keep things simple, if you do become aware of a taste or a smell, just note it as touch and see how it is a sensation that happens when a substance touches the body. For the most part, your overwhelming experience, especially on the cushion will be made up of Seeing, Touching, Feeling, Hearing and Thinking.

I'd like to talk to you a little bit about how the senses and thinking mix and mingle to create your experience. This is a very important aspect of the practice. Most people walking around take the combination of sensory experience and thinking and turn it into a conceptual experience – by thinking and labeling that combination as a stable, unchanging experience. We talked a bit about how that happens with anger. Think about eating at a restaurant you like. You order your favorite meal and enjoy all the sensory experiences that come with the taste of the meal (remember we're calling taste "touch"). Your thoughts say things like "I love this meal" which creates more good feelings in your body. These loop back and you think about how satisfied you are with the restaurant. Afterwards you feel satisfied (more pleasant body sensations). Inside of all these good body sensations are tiny little vibrations of feelings. And in the course of an hour long meal a conservative estimate of thoughts would probably be somewhere around 100. The next day a friend asks "How was dinner?" and you respond with "It was great!"

I think by now you can begin to see how all experience is a combination of sensory experience and thinking that can easily get all tangled up because we don't stop to spend time to really look at it. For the sake of simplicity, we conceptualize the hour long meal with many sensations and thoughts into 3 words – "It was great!" And if we have a meal that has some good points but also some unpleasantness we might say "It was Ok." Meals with overwhelming unpleasant body sensations (food not pleasing to the palate, thoughts about how bad the food is) are described as "It sucked!"

Our simple goal with meditation is to untangle the individual components of momentary experience and look at each one as they become prominent in our experience. Shinzen Young calls this Conquer and Divide. This becomes a powerful tool because teasing apart the body sensations and thinking that make up an unpleasant experience can help us better deal with that experience. Body sensations can be handled easier when separated from thought. Thinking is clearer when not clouded by powerful body sensations or emotions. So you could think of the goal of mindfulness to take all experiences, much like the "it was great" or "it sucked" experience above and unpack and track the ongoing sensations and thoughts.

We have used the terms pleasant and unpleasant a lot so far. There are a few reasons for that. First, they are fairly neutral terms to refer to what we'll call different flavors of experience. To the individual, he may be drawn to certain sensations and retreat from other sensations depending on many factors. Drama can be described as a person drawn to unpleasant situations – ultimately deriving some kind of pleasant sensation (often attention). But the thing to get here is that while we're on the cushion, the best practice is to drop this notion of good or bad, pleasant or unpleasant. These are ultimately judgments made by the mind. For the time we're on the cushion, we note without regard to whether something is pleasant or unpleasant. After just a little bit of practice, you'll be able to see how much your mind influences this judgment.

Pleasant body sensations can be a great tool for accessing deep levels of concentration. In fact, using blissful states and building on them will make up a lot of what you learn in this course. From a practical standpoint, feeling good is a good thing. But from an ultimate standpoint, it's just a thing without any inherent meaning. We talk about this more in the next book, but I've found the following distinction useful .You can split your experience of life up into 2 categories. The first category is the practical. Imagine you're playing Monopoly. If the whole time you're playing Monopoly you keep yelling that it's all a game, that none of this matters, than you're just being obnoxious. You play the game full out, you take the rules seriously and you try to win. But at any time, you're also able to step away from the board with the knowledge that it is all just a game, and that the rules and judgments of the game are all just made-up. This can be especially useful when the game isn't going well for you. When you're on the cushion, you're basically stepping away from the Monopoly board for a little while. When things get tough during the game, you'll have a way to access a simpler place free of the drama of the "game."

Before we get into the nuts and bolts of the practice, there are 3 powerful assumptions that can help your practice in the beginning. Again, it's not that these are meant to be taken as absolute truth, it's just that applying this model seems to help you get into the right mindset before practice.

In Buddhist psychology, it is assumed that you can only ever experience one thing at a time. But the mind gets so quick at experiencing that multiple senses seem to be happening at the same time. As your practice, it will seem like you're aware of sounds while you're "seeing, seeing, seeing." That is Ok, but for our purposes, we'll be focusing on the most prominent sensory experience at any given moment of noting. You may be "seeing, seeing, seeing" when the sound of a dog barking next door becomes the most prominent sensory experience. Keeping this idea that you're only ever aware of one thing at a time helps you to worry less about missing other things happening in your sensory experience.

This one relates to #1. It helps to pretend that the only thing in the world is what you're currently experiencing. That there isn't anything outside of your experience or your 6 senses of the world. This helps to put you in the moment, focus on the present and not worry so much about what's going on in the rest of the world. This little trick has definitely helped me to stay focused and minimize thoughts about things that will happen or have happened. What is happening right now is what is happening in your experience. Similarly, this helps to prevent thoughts of the past or planning for the future. If you have trouble with this, thinking that your experience is always right now seems to help. If you think about it, when tomorrow comes, it will just be right now again. And yesterday was just another moment of right now that has already happened. Try this on and see if it helps to ground you in the present.

This one may be a little hard to grasp at first but after some practice will become clear. This little thought helped me eventually pop after I was practicing for quite some time. So I'll just leave this here, if it doesn't make any sense, don't worry. **A thought or a body sensation can never observe another thought or body sensation.** What this means is that there are no "you" thoughts that are overseeing the other thoughts you have. With regards to body sensations, a lot of people tend to report their sense of awareness is felt mostly in the back of the head or the tops of the shoulders. This is the mind associating certain body sensations as being the sense of self more than other sensations. For a pointer on this one, I like the Alan Watts description of the self as being very similar to the appearance of a candle flame. When you look at it, it seems solid but we all know that it is a constant flickering of light that makes the candle appear solid and constant. Try to think of all the sensations and thoughts that make up what you normally think of "you" as similar to the flickering candle flame appears solid. It really helps to enter a meditation session with the mind primed to this idea of flickering body sensations and thoughts. Try it out and see how that feels.

Ok, we have gone over a lot of material for now. I've tried to keep it simple, but it's still a lot. This is the culmination of years of study and practice. These tips will get you started on the right foot and help you avoid a lot of the mistakes I made. Don't worry, with this foundation, you'll be practicing more efficiently and with better results than 95% of the people who "try" to meditate. We'll be making progress quickly once you have the groundwork down. So review what we've gone over so far and I'll see you in the next chapter where we start the actual practice.

Chapter 12: How To Meditate: Practical Exercises

How do you learn to be good at meditation? Frankly, there are many times when our minds just wander from what we should be concentrating on. In mindfulness meditation, the idea is to train your mind through practiced breathing. While doing this, you should pay attention to the thoughts which seem to drive your attention away from what you are concentrating on. Over time, this practice aids in building your attention muscles. Sounds simple, right?

However, mindfulness meditation is not that easy. It calls for patience from the meditator as they need to take time to master the art. Following the many meditation benefits which have been discussed, it is important for you to make meditation a habit. Indeed, this is one of the pillars of meditation which has been previously discussed in chapter 2. This section takes a more practical approach to how you can meditate.

Meditation: Theory Embodiment

The posture you take while meditating matters a great deal. With regards to mindfulness, this is an activity that can be practiced anywhere. Whether you are sitting, walking, or communicating with other people, you can choose to be mindful about the environment around you. Meditation focuses on mindfulness. When meditating, you are practicing mindfulness. You are training your attention muscles to be conversant of the body, sensations, mental states, and other mental processes. Nonetheless, this doesn't necessarily mean that your attention will be moving back and forth from the body to the mind and vice versa. However, being mindful means that you are fully aware of these foundations without having to wander.

Self-awareness is holistic in nature. This means that focusing on the mind will also require you to be cognizant of the body and other sensations. Basically, it revolves around the window that you prefer looking into. When our meditation is coupled with mindfulness, it means that we are in a better position to recognize our feelings, energies, and motivations. Undeniably, this is worthwhile because it is deep beneath the mind that we can awaken the giant within us.

Effectively penetrating the strata of the mind requires patience and practice. From the word go, this will demand that you should not get distracted by the thoughts flowing in and out of your mind. Certainly, when meditating, you can be sure that there are burdensome feelings and thoughts which will flow to your mind. The idea is not to get caught up in these thoughts. You simply need to identify that you are aware of them.

A practical way of bringing the mind to concentrate on the here and now is by paying attention to body sensations. This is a good place to start as it gives you a solid base of your self-awareness. The notion of living in the moment might sound pretty straightforward. Unfortunately, this is not always the case as most of our attention is usually focused on something else. We find ourselves talking with other people, but we are actually thinking of how you will arrive home without getting late. Our minds are easily distracted by thoughts simply because we grant unnecessary power to the mind.

One positive effect of mindfulness is a relaxed body. Throughout our day-to-day lives, there are daily stressors that we have to go through. This is what our mind and body have to go through every day. However, when the body is relaxed, it has a good impact on the heart since it can also relax. Conversely, a tensed body will make it challenging for the mind to meditate. This is because it cannot tap into the energy required for meditation purposes. Meditation, therefore, strives to put the body in a calm state where it can restore its energies in all areas thereby leading to an overall improvement in the health and wellbeing of the meditator.

The peace that comes with meditation occurs because, in the body's calm state, it is prevented from wandering around your past or your future. You don't have to worry about how your future will unfold and the activities that you are yet to do. Moreover, you learn to let go of the past. This means that your mind and body are both living in the present where there are peace, tranquility, and balance.

For you to reap the benefits of meditation, the right posture is imperative. This is because it allows the mind to circulate its calm energies all over. It is worth noting that this goes beyond your outer appearance. Basically, your posture should guarantee that your body is free from tensions both inside and outside. In other words, your body should be in a balanced state where it can easily recognize anything that tries to bring about an imbalance.

Consequently, sitting in the right posture doesn't necessarily imply that you should force your body into it. Rather, this is something that should be achieved by the body and the mind. It is a practice where the mind massages your attention to stay alert. So, it is vital that you give yourself time to understand that your posture is more than just sitting upright.

Sitting Meditation

The first step towards your meditation practice is learning how to sit. Using a chair or a cushion, sit on the floor. Cross your legs if you choose to sit on the floor. On the other hand, if you use a chair, you should ensure that your spine is upright. This means that your back should not lean on the chair. To achieve an upright posture, you can use a pillow to give your spine the right spinal axis. The important thing to ensure is that your spine should not be in any form of pressure as this will prevent it from fully supporting the body. The right posture guarantees that energy flows freely and smoothly from the body to the mind.

Aligning Your Body Structure

Again, when using a chair, it is vital that you make sure the soles of your feet comfortably reach the ground. This means that if the chair is too tall for you, try to find another one which is shorter. Your thighs should also rest cozily on the seat. Your feet should be kept shoulders width apart. If you choose to sit on the floor, cross your legs to achieve a sitting position where one is tucked under the other. If you are not flexible enough, just cross your legs in any way you feel comfortable. The essential thing here is to maintain an upright position.

Once you are certain that your body is in an upright position, put your arms to rest on your crossed legs. Any tension from the shoulders to the arms should be allowed to drain straight to the ground. The weight of the body should also be allowed to balance evenly on the ground.

Sweeping the Body

Once you have achieved the right sitting posture, the next thing to do is to sweep your attention to the body. Why is this important? Well, it goes without saying that you can easily slip out of the posture that you have achieved. This means that this can distract your attention. Therefore, your attention should be on the body and not on the posture for you to gain the perfect level of awareness.

A huge benefit of body-sweeping is that it strengthens mindfulness. This is achieved by carrying the bodily experiences to the mind. Therefore, clear attention about the body is gained by the mind without actually forcing it. Through evaluation, you can bring out any indifferent attitudes and reinstate them with care and mindfulness. For instance, your awareness can be evaluated by asking: Where is my neck? Or where is my right hand right now? Your feelings can also be gauged by asking: How am I feeling right now? What is happening there, inside my mind? Such "checking in" can really be beneficial during meditation.

The notion of checking in can also be identified as body scan meditation. What you are trying to do is to create a high level of awareness about your body. This means that you should be aware of the ground you are sitting or stepping on. The process should be done step by step. From head to toe, you should also consider the most basic part of your body, including being aware of your small and large toe. Remember, you are not judging anything while doing this. Checking in is all a matter of knowing the body inside your body. Just put your focus on noticing.

Walking Meditation

Let's face it, there are particular activities which have forced most of us to live lives behind the desk. This means that anything else that you might want to do will appear counteractive. However, mindfulness doesn't have to be perceived that way since you can do it while engaging in other activities that you are accustomed to.

When walking, simply assume a natural walking pace. Your hands should be placed anywhere as long as you are comfortable. You can give your concentration a boost by counting the number of steps you take to 10 and starting over again and again. If you will be practicing walking meditation in an enclosed room, take small steps. When you reach ten, take a pause, then turn around gently and with intention.

With every step that you take, your attention should be on the rising and falling of your feet on the ground. As you do this, you should also take note of other body movements which are affected by how you walk. Welcome anything else that seems to draw your attention from your walking. Acknowledge its existence, but don't do anything about it. Bring your mind back to focus and concentrate on your walking. Sure, your mind will keep wandering, but your aim is to gently bring it back to pay attention to what should be its center of attention: your walking.

Essential Factors to Consider When Meditating

Successful meditation comes with practice. This is not something that will take you a single day to learn everything. What's more, besides reading books such as this, it is crucial that you do it practically for you to gain maximum benefits. There are several essentials that you should bear in mind when meditating.

Use the Right Posture

A rule of thumb that you should always consider each time you meditate is whether you have taken the right posture. Whether you sit on a chair or on the floor, the right upright posture should always be maintained. This will confirm that energy flows smoothly from your body to the mind.

First, Meditate with Eyes Open

When meditating for the first time, it is vital that you practice this with your eyes open. This will help you increase the awareness aspect. Meditating with the eyes closed is highly recommended. However, it might be difficult for newbies to fully concentrate as their minds can easily drift.

Focus on Your Presence

In ordinary circumstances, focusing on yourself is hard. Nevertheless, with meditation, you can achieve this by first paying attention to bodily sensations. Start by focusing on how you breathe. If possible, make a count of how you are breathing to boost your attention. Slowly, allow your mind to take over this counting process. After that, proceed to checking in. Recognize every part of your body and how you are feeling at the moment.

Ideally, this allows you to live in the present.

Don't Fall for Your Emotions

The aim of meditation mindfulness is not to fight your emotions. Rather, it seeks to raise your level of consciousness that you are fully aware of what is going on in your mind and body. So, instead of fighting your emotions, allow them to flow as you label them. They could be feelings of sadness, happiness, or joy. Keep labeling them, but don't get caught up with them. Remember, there is nothing that you should do about them. Gradually, your mind should be drifted back to your subject of focus depending on the meditation technique you use.

Meditate in Silence

It will be impossible to achieve peace within you when your external environment is noisy. Therefore, the right environment to meditate will be a quiet place. This warrants that you minimize the number of distractions preventing you from achieving focus.

Practically, mindfulness meditation is not as difficult as you might have been thinking. Nevertheless, it requires patience from your end. For you to be a good meditator, you have to do it daily. You have to strengthen your attention muscles every day. So, it's not just about assuming the right posture or using the best mindfulness technique. There is more to meditation than just that from what has been discussed.

Chapter 13: Mindfulness Techniques

Normally our mind is like a machine. It keeps working 24/7. It is in constant motion of thinking, feeling, flitting from one thought to another endlessly. Due to this continuous motion the mind becomes tired, dull and slow. Awareness may peep through all this but the negative thoughts are higher and they simply subdue the awareness. Noisy thoughts and gloomy emotions cloud our thinking and we land up in a mess. You become edgy and upset without any reason. Anger peeps in and when you're angry there is no room for happiness. This is when you need to practice mindfulness. Where there is mindfulness there is peace, calm and joy. You're completely aware of what is happening. This awareness helps you to shed the negative thoughts and your mind finds balance.

As with any meditation session, you need to get into a relaxed and comfortable position, eyes closed, and then commence with deep nasal breathing, focusing your thoughts on the breathing to ease yourself into a meditative state. Once you feel that you are calmed by your breathing and that your breath is under your rhythmic control, then you can move on to focusing on your own body, a part at a time. There are four steps to practice mindfulness. They are preparation, relaxation, mindfulness and stillness.

Step 1 - Preparation
Step 2 - Relaxation
Step 3 - Mindfulness
Step 4 - Stillness

Preparation is about all the practical details of posture, place and time to meditate, attitude and how to begin your meditation practice. Posture is important in mindfulness meditation so that the energy will flow better. A comfortable seating position should be selected; it does not matter whether it is lotus, Burmese or Seiza positions. Let your hands rest on top of your thighs. The palms of your hand should be on a downward position. Choose a place in your home where you feel comfortable. Meditate at the same place every day. It shouldn't be that you keep changing your place of meditation. So select a favorite corner where you particularly feel comfortable and sit there every day. You can also meditate out in the open. By the sea or on top of a mountain or in your neighborhood garden where you've chirping birds and waves for company. Your mind automatically gets calm and serene. Peaceful surroundings are essential for practicing any form of meditation, especially mindfulness. The endeavor is to create a space in your home or outside where you can feel safe and secured to meditate in peace. It'll be your 'go to' place, away from the outside world where you can introspect and shed all your unnecessary and unwanted thoughts. This place will help you to heal, grow and bloom into a positive, calm and satisfied person. Some people are lucky to have a room for meditating. Keep that space de-cluttered. Maximum you can keep in that room is an aromatic candle, a vase with flowers and minimum furniture. Keep it as your meditation room so that the moment you enter the room peace engulfs you. There are many ways of making the approach to meditation as joyful as possible. You can transform the most ordinary of rooms into an intimate sacred space, an environment where every day you go to meet with your true self with all the joy and happy habit of one old friend greeting another.

Another aspect in preparation is the clothes you wear. Avoid wearing tight fitting clothes while meditating. Wear loose clothes that will help you to sit in peace for a while. Formal clothes and jeans are a definite no, no. Remember mindfulness is all about breathing. So wear clothes that you're comfortable to breathe in. another aspect is a mat to sit on. Instead of sitting on your bed or sofa, it'll be ideal to squat on the floor on top of a mat.

Posture is very important in meditation. Sitting cross legged with hands on the knees (padmasana / lotus pose) is perfect for meditation. The spine is straight and the back is erect. Your head looks ahead and hands are stretched. This position helps to concentrate on a single object while meditating as your body is balanced. Mindfulness is about concentrating on your breathing. Whether you sit up or lie down the aim is to have symmetry in your posture so that your body is balanced on both sides.

Jenny, a banker was totally stressed after a hard day at work. Meeting clients, managing funds, reaching targets put a lot of responsibility on her thin shoulders. She had constant headaches and lack of sleep till one of her colleagues mentioned about mindfulness to her. She met with a Guru and learnt to meditate. After a couple of months Jenny decided to meditate every day at home. She selected the smaller room as meditation room in her swanky 2 BHK apartment. She kept a chair and a small center table in that room. She used her grandmother's crochet table cloth for that center table. She kept a crystal candle stick above it which was also heirloom. The table cloth and candle stick made her nostalgic and reminded her of the love and wonderful times she shared with her grandmother. She also had a yoga mat and a vase in one corner. She refilled the vase once in two days with fresh flowers. Her meditation room gave her inner peace as soon as she entered the room, as it transported her to the days she spent in loving care of her grandmother. The room more or less became a holy place to Jenny. Whenever she thought of her room there was a smile on her face. The fact that she had a meditation room where she could connect with her pleasant past and remain peaceful made her rush back home every day.

Jenny lighted the candle everyday as she sat down to meditate. The glow from the candle gave her peace and the room was tranquil with the glowing candle and fresh flowers. When you start your day with a simple ten minute meditation in such a peaceful atmosphere your entire day passes off peacefully. This room made her feels good and she looked forward to her meditation routine.

Relaxation has everything to do with your mind and body. Now that you've established a regular place to meditate you've think about how to relax both your body and mind. Tell yourself that you're going to be fine and all your problems will be solved and you'll be free from worries. As you tell this to yourself you'll feel the tension leaving your body and you feel relaxed. As your mind is calm it becomes clearer and you're able to assess your situation with clarity. You let go of unwanted thoughts and think about the now. When you're relaxing you need to be aware of where you're and in which posture you're. Then slowly tell yourself to relax each and every part of your body. Here it is important to mention that you can keep your eyes closed. Start from your feet and move upwards to each and every part of your body. From feet you move to your legs then thighs, hips, hands, fingers, shoulders and then move upwards to your face. This is known as progressive muscle relaxation (PMR) exercise. Ask yourself how your body is feeling today? Are your feet fine? Is your hip aching? Here it is important to be positive. Don't question in a negative manner. Relax into relaxation and be content to notice how your body is feeling today.

Let go of all expectations during this exercise. The aim of this exercise is to perform without any judgment. Even if you're in pain tell yourself that it should go away. Simply push it away from your thoughts. This way your body will also respond positively to your mind. The PMR exercise makes you aware of each and every part of your body that'll help you to relax and enjoy this journey. Our mission is to relax the body that automatically calms the mind and takes you into the meditative state where you're fully mindful (aware) of yourself. Once you reach this state of relaxation the body and mind are in balance with each other.

The secret is to assume an open interest as to how your body feels at that particular moment, as you're performing this exercise and to accept that this is the truth of the matter, this is how it is, and then to use these techniques to lead your body into a deeper, more serene and relaxed state. The truth is it actually works. It's simple and direct. You spend 10 to 15 seconds on a specific part of your body and know how it feels and then move on to the next part to explore a different sensation. Your curiosity to know how each part of your body feels makes you to think about each and every part and that mindfulness (awareness) aids in relaxation.

When you're thinking about your muscles they contract and make you aware that you're thinking about them. For example if you're thinking about your calf muscle then it automatically contracts and your mind helps you to identify that particular muscle group. Then you command your mind to relax it. This way you contract and relax each and every muscle in your body. While doing this you deliberately contract and relax the muscle there by removing the tension present in it. You'll notice that the muscle is softening and the tension created is going away. While releasing, the left over tension also leaves the body and you relax completely. Once this exercise of contracting, relaxing and then 'letting go' of the tension becomes a habit, you automatically 'let go' of tension while not meditating also.

Here's an example: When Rich was given the pink slip he thought his whole world had come to a standstill. His beautiful wife Rihanna and his two wonderful kids, his faithful dog came into his mental picture. How am I going to protect them all? How am I going to pay the mortgage, car loan and other bills?? He could feel his blood pressure shooting up. Since he was regularly into meditation he simply pushed away such thoughts and relaxed himself by letting go of these thoughts. Quietly he left office and reached home and went straight into his meditation room. Soon he felt the familiar feeling of security engulf him as he entered his favorite abode. Instinctively he knew he'll survive this….He sat in his favorite chair and took the shawl and spread it on his legs, as he always did. He felt 'at home' and peaceful. He meditated for a while. Later he told his wife about his job loss and she comforted him by saying that "everything happens for the good".

After a week of staying at home and browsing for offers Rich decided to offer his services as a freelancer online at several market places. Soon the jobs started coming and Rich's confidence grew. He could spend more time meditating and that helped him to think with clarity and precision. He calculated his finances and realized that he can manage to pay off the bills and mortgage as well, if he cuts some corners. He sold his new Pontiac and bought a second hand car for a lesser price. His auto loan was closed and monthly outgoing on car insurance also came down. He used his credit card sparingly and ate only at home. Since he was a work at home dad he could spend quality time with the kids and Rihanna. He also helped her in household chores and life seemed better to him now. After a couple of months Rich's jobs increased and he had to hire a couple of guys to help him with the work. They too worked from their homes and using Skype and Google docs Rich was able to monitor the work. Rich realized that from an individual freelancer he had to move to become a company. He needed an office and so shared office space with a friend. He tackled his finances brilliantly and soon he was running his own company. This clearly shows that when you're calm and relaxed you can think clearly and take wise decisions.

Instead of fretting and stressing himself as well as his family Rich meditated and kept himself composed. He was also positive that something wonderful is sure to happen. He intuitively knew that he would succeed if he kept his calm and remain grounded. Meditation increases the level of intuition in the individual.

Mindfulness is the third step where you're aware of your thoughts. It makes you mindful of your surroundings as well as your inner thoughts. Once your body is relaxed after preparation and relaxation you become aware of your thoughts. Mindfulness is like waking up to life. When you're in an agitated state you forget to look around you or think with clarity. A mindless life becomes dull and chaotic. Have you ever noticed a sunset? Or appreciated a child's laughter? With the practice of mindfulness you'll start to notice these things and learn to enjoy the simple pleasures of life.

Mindfulness develops attention, concentration and the ability to simply be present with little or no future, past or goal orientation. Mindfulness practice slows down the forward projection of the thinking mind, which is overly committed to achieving, getting, having, holding and protecting. Mindfulness practice slows down the momentum of the ego or the personality, and allows contact with a deeper, stiller, quieter part of one's true nature.

Breath is the bridge between your body and mind.

The basic principle of mindfulness is attention to breathing. Our breath is what keeps us alive on this planet. There is no need to change your breathing pattern. Simply observe it. This is not a breathing exercise. The aim is to be aware of your breath rather than controlling it. Breath is what keeps us alive. That is why it is called

'Prana' in Sanskrit which means life's force. If there is no prana then the body is just a corpse. It is prana that keeps us alive. So you need to concentrate on your breathing. No need to alter it. Simply observe your breath. Be aware of how the air is inhaled and exhaled. Concentrate on the place above the upper lip and below the nostrils. You can feel the cold air entering your nostrils. When you exhale you'll feel the hot air coming out. This heat is generated by your body and this is energy. The cold air gets converted inside you to propel your body parts to be in optimum shape. While breathing, you'll feel your stomach and chest muscles contract and release. Listen to the rhythmic feel of your breath as it is the essential life giver for growth. Attention to the breath can produce a deep respect and appreciation for the breath of life.

If you feel that your thoughts are wandering away from your breath, bring it back to concentrate on your breathing.

This will help you to relax and be mindful of your surroundings and inner self as well. You're free of judgment and free of reaction. In doing so you're able to think with rationality and that helps you in achieving success. This is a very simple process where the effects are powerful.

Stillness As we become more mindful, we learn to give our attention more fully to whatever we are doing in the present moment, we notice a fundamental truth: there is activity in our life and there is stillness. Once you've prepared yourself for relaxing and being mindful of your breath your body and mind are in balance with each other. Now you should try to control your thoughts. When mind is still then there is bliss, joy and satisfaction. Controlling your thoughts is a very essential part of mindfulness. You become non-judgmental and focus completely on what you're doing. You can also remain still in the mind with a room full of people. If you can disassociate your thoughts from your surroundings then you can achieve stillness. Controlling your thoughts and training them to think what you want to is the ultimate aim of stillness. With continuous practice of meditation and mindfulness you achieve the state of stillness.

You may take up meditation to manage stress or to heal physically and mentally, to find more peace and balance in your life, to be more efficient at work or to perform better at sport, or to be a nicer person. All these things are real possibilities as a consequence of regular meditation, and it makes good sense to begin meditation with any of these intentions in mind. But the reason why meditation is the greatest gift you can give yourself—or, if you can, give to your loved one —is that meditation introduces us to our innermost nature, the truth of who we really are. You look within yourself and ask the question 'Who am I?' You find answers to questions that've been plaguing you for a long time. Finally you feel that you've come a full circle. In mindfulness you need to concentrate on each and every body part one by one. By doing this you become aware of yourself. Once you've focused on each part of your body like right leg, right knee, right hand, fingers, right eye, right ear and then move on to the left side. Now open your eyes and focus on a single object in the room. It can be anything like a flower vase or pen stand. Try to focus on it for half a minute and then turn away. While doing this keep your concentration on your breathing and your body parts. This triple focus makes you aware of your own self, your breathing and your surroundings. You can use an audio cd to guide you through this.

Resistance to meditate

Some people sleep during meditation. This is a form of resistance in our brain. The mind is continuously planning, plotting, judging, worrying and doesn't wish to be still. But with the practice of meditation you'll reach the state of calm and nothingness. While initially practicing meditation/ mindfulness you may have unwanted thoughts entering your mind and refusing to go away. This is quite natural. Look at your thoughts as if it is happening to someone else and learn to push it away. With practice you'll be able to push away your thoughts and reach a state of peace.

Chapter 14: Putting It All Together

You cannot stop to meditate every moment of the day, but you can learn to live in the moment and to maximize your appreciation of the world and what it offers you. Mindful people are able to feel humility. They are also able to feel happy inside. They know the difference between pride and humbleness but they treat both beasts the same, without judgment and that's going to be the tough lesson for anyone new to this lifestyle.

You can practice mindfulness meditation to help you to energize yourself when you have the time, but you can practice mindfulness all of the time. Of course, you will find yourself experiencing negative moments, but don't judge them or dwell on them. That negative moment will soon be gone and will be followed by a positive moment if you let it.

Let's try and demonstrate how thoughts are fleeting and how one moment can change suddenly as something happens in life to force change.

Supposing that you are angry inside. Your thoughts are completely negative and you have thoughts racing through your mind. You will see just how quickly these can disappear when I use this example. In the next moment, you hear that a friend is dying of cancer and needs to talk to you. Instead of carrying on feeling angry, it's natural to put your feelings to one side and deal with the urgency of the other situation.

Thus if you continue to feel angry, the friend who has cancer isn't going to get the best you can offer them. If, however, you use mindfulness, you can see the negativity of anger and be aware of it, but also be aware of it being fleeting and something that will pass. Don't judge it, don't analyze it or it will follow you into the next moment.

Instead, accept it as is. It's anger and the next moment you get may not give you that feeling of anger. If you can start to think of life in this way, you begin to find a real contentment in your life that you never had before, simply because you are not letting negative influences have any effect on the way that you see them. They are simply moments and they are what they are. They are only more than that if you allow them to be.

It is a very good idea to follow the easy patterns where you can be mindful, such as when using the senses. Taste your food. Savor it and enjoy it more. You will improve your digestion and will potentially slow down because you will hear your own body's needs better. Eating food quickly while being unaware of the sensation of eating really wastes your time and doesn't help you to feel better about yourself.

If you can combine relaxation exercises, meditation practice and practice in your day to day life, your life becomes more vital, more energetic and more satisfying. That's when you know for sure that you have it right and that you are gaining something from the practice of mindfulness.

Do you gulp your coffee for a quick caffeine kick? Savor it. Take a sip and let the coffee slide over your taste buds. Feel the taste and enjoy the coffee more. Similarly with chocolate, let it melt on the tongue. Let it open up all of your senses because when you are mindful, it really will. Mindfulness is a wonderful place for your mind to be in. The opportunities that it offers are something to celebrate.

Chapter 15: The Problem Of The Present

Everyone has a dream that can be realized ... Until the end of this week! But most of you lack a lifetime for this! – A "passerby."
How many pages are usually open in the browser of a regular computer? I have about seven open on average. It's on the desktop. Next to it is usually an open laptop. And in it the same amount. And how many programs are simultaneously launched? And the tablet is still there. And chat rooms in social networks? Skype? And chats on the mobile phone? That is, sorry, the smartphone. How many people are in contact with us at the same time? What were we going to do when we turned on the computer? For a second on Facebook/YouTube, and then work hard? A second in Facebook can last up to several hours, and sometimes days.
Then came a few e-mails, someone wrote in the chat, someone commented on the post, and someone else marked the photo

as liked, someone posted something so unacceptable to the network that you should immediately evaluate, but here again laid out new cats, now more children, new posts in our Facebook group, oh my, we need to write something like this, how not to explain to the scribe that. They are rushing news - politics, wars, crises, presidents, rumors, movie stars, facts, cars, conjectures, computers. And again Telegram, WhatsApp, Instagram, Twitter, Viber ... a million different notifications. No matter what. It is important that around us, there are thousands of different distractions that lead the war for our attention.

How many times did you have to be distracted by the phone while reading this text? Or wanted to distract? Or check on how is it on Instagram. How many likes did a newly published photo get? Or I suddenly remembered that I wanted to write an answer to that message quickly. Or maybe there are just other distractions.

We are all different, but for everyone, there is something different that helps not to be in reality.

When there are so many factors distracting and occupying attention and intelligence, it is surprising that we generally have time to do something at work. Caesar never dreamed of such multitasking!

And then - the same thing after work, because the work is not the main thing, there is also a personal one. The way home is on the phone screen, we are happy owners of new, modern gadgets, with a bright screen, a powerful processor. A happy opportunity presented by caring developers to do several things at the same time. How can you dare to miss such a thing?! So what, what's behind the wheel? Anyway, traffic jams.

In our houses, how many channels do our televisions have? Someone, in addition to this, also has the analog paradise of a rustling newspaper or the glossy gloss of a new magazine without distracting from the TV. Some messages from work came it is necessary to look urgently. It was also necessary to read the postponed for the evening: an article, a note, a letter. Be sure to eat simultaneously.

And these are only informational "distractions." This is without the factor of other people. Our parents, our families - wives, husbands, children, our animals, who also need communication.

The boss wrote something. Or a business partner. Or If we live in two hemispheres, where some are friends in Europe / Asia, and some in America, then this can continue at night. Yes, and we, too, are not badly sewn. We write, respond, celebrate, constantly tugging at other people, believing that they are obliged to respond to our messages, comments, and reposts immediately. Angry if this does not happen.

And a few years ago, if someone didn't immediately respond to the letter, that is, in the past minute, then-No one had much time to do with it.

When they do not answer us, they do not comment about us; they don't like us, they don't write to us. Then we yes, we are frustrated; we are dissatisfied.

When the opposite happens, it happens as if some pleasant chemicals are released into the mind. Wrote. Posted. Noted on the photo. A tweet has been quoted a certain number of times. A letter from the online store only you, we give this discount. Happiness! And the circle begins again: no, this is bad, even lonely, empty. Things are fine; joyfully, I'm in touch! With me in touch! Pay attention to me. I am needed!

Being in touch is easy and pleasant. And we feel these feelings immediately as soon as we go online.

Another important feeling is ownership. After all, everything is here and now. I am also with everyone. We are together. I am part of something big, even worldwide!

By the way, there are still such people (they are very few, few) who have no email address, no smartphone, no social network account, or Skype. We look at them as strange, incomprehensible, near, alien, suspicious. They are not with us. And here we are again in the network. We do not want to be looked at us in the same way. Again at the source of information. Again we want to be aware. We do not want to be outsiders.

Society requires us to connect permanently. Suddenly it became like this: when there is a connection, it is excellent; when there is no connection, it is bad.

The scheme is similar to the use of any substances. First, immediately well, then, after a while, without this, it is no longer possible. And from this is unbearably bad. However, in the case of substances, the price of changes eventually becomes overwhelming, and the destruction is too obvious to deny them, and indeed, it is against the law.

In the case of information dependence, everything is not so ...

What?

Was it said "addiction"?

And can it be called otherwise? The earlier morning began with a cigarette and a newspaper, and now with a cigarette and a smartphone. People quit smoking, but who will give up the smartphone? It seems to be the same. Only new technologies have changed the look of the newspaper. But in a cafe, couples on a date or just friends/colleagues/acquaintances are sitting opposite each other, and everyone reads something on their phone. It is possible, of course, that they write each other messages. But a man in a public toilet is standing, holding a phone with one hand and reading someone's Facebook status, and a second hand at this time.

Wildness? But if one of us has not yet reached this, it is only because he is unable to bring a television or other means of distraction from the ordinary in a public toilet. Ten years ago, in England, long before Facebook and iPhones. It was noticed that most of the phone networks were killed precisely when they were recessed in toilets. And then people could only read SMS. But good. A simple test. Highly.

Try to decide not to touch your phone/tablet / TV/computer for the next ... say, thirty minutes. Come back to read later - try just to sit, relax, drink tea/coffee, go out for a walk, or smoke, or close your eyes, but do nothing else.

Either you didn't do that at all, or it was very hard. Almost impossible. As a rule, an irresistible desire to check what new had appeared appears in half a minute. Silence, peace, and loneliness are terrible and dangerous things, leading to an inevitable collision with yourself. To be in silence is incomprehensible, unpleasant, empty. Emptiness is one of the biggest enemies of modern human consciousness. Being out of communication is equal to absence in life, equal to being lonely. Loneliness is tantamount to death.

What is the result? Dependence on the flow of information. Dependence on "being in touch." Dependence on instant satisfaction with the "like" on the reaction to the next "urgent" news. We suddenly began to consider all this as life, and the greater the flow of information, the more acutely we experience "life." But only each of us knows deep down that this is an illusion. So they go day after day, week after week, year after year. Then, occasionally meeting each other, we recall old, almost forgotten dreams, aspirations, ideas. Or, in the infrequent moments of quiet nostalgia for lost opportunities and unfulfilled desires, we think how to realize them once, but just don't find the time. As a result, we return to the good old universe "here if." And then we suddenly realize that the years have passed, the condition "if only" does not work anymore, except "in another life." In which even if we get, it is not a fact that we will not make all these mistakes again. More precisely, not "mistakes," but an error. Since it is one, we do not live here and now.

The modern world, to which we were so eager, suddenly did the unexpected - our minds were given new options not to be in the present moment. The hypnotic effect of information flow. The opportunity to continue not to wake up.

The only question is - is it true that this is all really a problem? And really, what is the problem that we are so dependent on? Dependence on electricity, hot water, cars, air conditioners, for example. And there is nothing wrong with that. Well, yes, we have forgotten how to survive without warmth in winter and coolness in summer. We are accustomed to fresh and do not tolerate the smell and type of unclean people; we don't carry warm things in the cold and light in the heat. We have changed a lot since the beginning of the era of machines. But no one says that achievements must be abandoned. It would be like a call to go into the forest to live in a hole by the lake.

However, multitasking, under the conditions of which we suddenly found ourselves, is too multitasking, is not it? Often, as a result, we become incompetent to perform any one simple task in one separate period of time.

Chapter 16: Develop Your Self-Regulation

Self-regulation is the final important skill we are going to analyze when it comes to handling your emotions, your stress levels, and therefore being free to listen to your body. As adults we are able to pretty much do everything we want at any time we want as long as we are within logical boundaries and we don't harm others. For example, we don't need to go to work every day, the vast majority of people will go to jail for skipping a day or two from work. Or we can eat cake or pizza for breakfast if that is what we desire. So, why are we going to work every day and why we prefer to eat pizza or cake for breakfast? How do we force ourselves to endure working on a day that this is the last place we would like to be in? How do we keep ourselves from not indulging in an unhealthy breakfast and we go for the healthy choice?

To the above questions, the answer is self-regulation, a process that most people follow without even thinking this is what they are practicing at a precise moment. Self-regulation is a skill that has to do with controlling our emotions, behaviors, and thoughts in favor of achieving the goals we have set for the future. This is why we are able to control our impulses of not going to work or eating an unhealthy breakfast. In other words, we are taught to think before we act, we practice self-control. A person who has developed self-regulation skills can keep his or her emotions under control and resist indulging in impulsive behaviors that might end up harming them. They can also cheer themselves up whenever they are feeling down and they can also match their emotional as well as their behavioral responses to the demands of their environment.

The ability to self-regulate in adulthood comes from our childhood since it is an important skill, children need to be taught for their emotional maturity and their future social interactions as they grow to be adults. Emotional self-regulation is the ability of a person to control or influence his or her emotions by taking the necessary steps to get himself or herself out of a bad mood or destress. Behavioral self-regulation is the ability of a person to act on behalf of his or her long-term goal and interests in a wat that is connected with his or her values. For example, you may not want to go to work, but you decide to go because you need money to live and know that it will reflect badly on your future goals if you aim for a promotion or to put some money aside to make your dreams happen.

Self-regulation will help both a child and an adult to control his or her cognitive impulses to respond to an uncomfortable feeling or environmental threats. For example, as a child, you may have been prone to throwing tantrums and grown into an adult who has learned how to tolerate the emotions that made you uncomfortable without having to resort to the behavior you had adopted as a child. Now, you are able to control your urges to act on emotions that make you uncomfortable and trigger a response that you have deemed as bad.

Self-regulation is a process in which we must be cautious of our behavior, the things that influence it as well as the consequences our behavior has on ourselves and our surroundings. Values are extremely important because we must judge our behavior according to our own standards as well as the standards presented by our broader environment. Also, we must ponder sometimes about what we think of our own behavior and the different ways we deal when faced with an important situation or decision. Do we often give in to our impulses? Do we let our emotions control our behavior which often leads us to make many mistakes?

In other words, you should take a pause and take some time between what you feel and your actions. Taking the necessary time between those two will let you think everything you are dealing with through, form a plan, and wait until your plan can be executed and wait for the results to become apparent. Children, as well as adults, may not find those steps easy to follow, but the problems caused by lacking the self-regulation skills will make anyone who wants to better his or her life develop them.

For example, a child who does not practice self-regulation will give in to his or her anger and may even resort to hitting other children out of frustration and that, in turn, will make him less able to maintain friendships and will face reprimands from his or her school. Most children resort to bullying due to this fact. They are not able to control their emotions that correspond to actions along with other psychological problems they may face. As far as children are concerned, they must be taught self-regulation skills or they are going to face many difficulties in their adult lives with behaviors that are developed from childhood.

Many adults suffer from poor self-regulation skills and self-confidence because they weren't taught as children how to develop those necessary abilities. Adults who lack those skills will have trouble handling stress and their anger. They are more prone to developing a mental disorder and they will develop anxiety disorders due to the fact that they will not be able to control their anger and other emotions such as sadness and fear. They may not even have a developed value system that would allow them to act according to it and they will have trouble expressing themselves appropriately. For example, if an adult values achieving in academics, he or she will not let themselves slack off before a test, in contrast to someone who will do so if he hasn't learned self-regulation.

So, people face problems with self-regulation because their childhood was not ideal. He or she may have felt insecure and not as safe as they should. In other cases, where self-regulation problems were not caused by problematic childhood, the adult may not have followed the necessary strategies for managing feelings that would have made him or her uncomfortable. Self-regulation and self-control have a lot in common since they are very similar concepts. However, according to psychologist Stuart Shanker, they differ on two basic matters:

"Self-control is about inhibiting strong impulses; self-regulation is about reducing the frequency and intensity of strong impulses by managing stress-load and recovery. In fact, self-regulation is what makes self-control possible, or, in many cases, unnecessary."

Self-regulation is a more automatic process that happens in our subconscious unless a person chooses to monitor his or her behavior and feeling to control the self-regulation process. To further understand the concept of self-regulation, it is better to see what happens in action. Let us take a cashier who successfully remains calm and polite when he or she is berated from an angry customer for a situation he or she has no control over. Another example can be that of a child who does not throw a tantrum when he or she is told by the parents that he or she cannot have the desirable toy. A couple who is arguing about something important and decide to take some time to cool off can be another example of practicing self-regulation.

When it comes to listening to your body, an appropriate example can be when you are trying to lose weight in order for you to be the best, healthier part of yourself, and you go out with a friend at a restaurant. While your friend may eat everything he or she wants, you decide to stick with the healthier choice because you know that eating unhealthy food will push back and affect your goals.

What can you do though to develop your self-regulation abilities? The first thing you can do and we have already analyzed is practicing mindfulness. With mindfulness, you will be able to place some distance between your emotions and reactions and focus on relaxation and calmness. Another strategy you can follow and will allow you to enhance your self-regulation abilities is cognitive reappraisal or else cognitive reframing. Cognitive reappraisal includes changing your mindset, in other words, the way you think about things. To be more specific, during this method you will have to interpret again a difficult and stressful situation you had to endure in order to alter your emotional response to it.

An example of such a case can be the fact that your good friend had not contacted you in days or even does not return your texts and calls. That will make you feel neglected and you will probably stress about him or her avoiding you or that he or she doesn't want to speak with you ever again. With cognitive reappraisal, you will think that your friend may be really busy or is facing a problem with his or her own, instead of thinking that your friend hates you. If you practice cognitive reappraisal in your everyday life, you will be able to replace any negative emotions with positive ones and change your mindset for the better.

Some other effective strategies for self-regulation are acceptance of a situation and problem-solving skills, instead of avoidance, distraction, worrying, and suppression of emotions. The first step to self-regulation is to accept and recognize that people have a choice on how to react to every situation they face. More specifically, you have three options that include avoidance, attack, and approach. It is a fact that your feelings will lead to one path, but the truth is that you are not forced to listen to your feelings every time. You have control over them and behaving in a certain manner is your choice.

Then, you should monitor your body since this is the one which will give you the necessary clues about how you are feeling, especially in cases that your feelings are not apparent to you. For example, when your heart beats rapidly this may be a sign that you are entering a rage state or you are going through a panic attack. You should ask yourself if you are running away from difficult situations constantly. What are your emotions and your body's response during that time? Do you feel the need to scream in anger at someone who has hurt you or done something wrong? Will you get anything out of screaming your anger out or should you discuss the situation when you are calm? Start with building your boundaries and your value system rather than trying to suppress emotions. Try to see the larger picture and act in a way that will benefit you and the people around you.

Self-regulation is an integral part of emotional intelligence. According to Mayer's and Salovey's model of emotional intelligence, this ability is defined as:

"The ability to perceive emotions, to access and generate emotions so as to assist thought, to understand emotions and emotional knowledge, and to reflectively regulate emotions so as to promote emotional and intellectual growth"

According to expert Daniel Goleman, emotional intelligence is consisted of three parts, which are self-awareness, empathy, self-regulation, social skills, and internal motivation. Self-regulation, the ability to control or influence our emotions, is an essential part of emotional intelligence because the better we can understand and face our emotions and those of others, the better we will become to understanding the environment we find ourselves in and adapt to this environment which will result in pursuing our goals in a much easier way than before.

Usually, adults have problems practicing self-regulation at work because they are not able to handle their emotions under pressure. To better manage your emotions at work, you should do some breathing exercises; stay hydrated by drinking lots of water, eating healthy, and sleep at least eight hours a night. When you are trying to practice self-regulation, you should keep in mind some pointers that will help you succeed.

You should try to live your life with integrity by being a good role model for your family, friends, and to everyone, you associate yourself with. Live by the values you have adopted and try not to bend them for anyone. Be open to change and challenge yourself to deal with it in the best way that you can. If you find yourself struggling, work to improve your adaptation abilities and stay positive that you will succeed.

Identify what triggers certain behaviors by being aware of your strengths and weaknesses as well as what your limits are. When you pinpoint the triggers responsible for your bad behavior, try to change those behaviors by practicing meditation to stay focused and calm. Self-discipline is important when you want to achieve self-regulation. Work persistently towards your goals and that includes not reacting badly to every difficult situation you may face. If you react according to your emotions every time, you will face extreme setbacks that will make you lose any motivation to become what you always wished to be.

Take a step back from your thoughts and try to tackle the negative emotions associated with them, but never ignore your thoughts. Acknowledge them, analyze them, and try to solve the problems that are causing them. Letting go of negativity will open many opportunities for you and your mind will be clear to tackle effectively any task you will be given.

You will be able to think more clearly if you detach yourself from difficult situations and keep calm when you are asked to solve a problem. You will be able to consider the consequences of your actions. For example, what would happen if you did not follow self-regulation on a pressing matter and gave in to anger and frustration? Would the results of each course of action be different or would they remain the same? Keep in mind that there are also long-term consequences to your choices that will affect your future. If you keep thinking of this, you will be able to place some distance between your emotions and your actions.

Believing in yourself is the base of all self-regulation practices. You will need to work on your self-confidence and focus on your successes in life instead of pondering on your mistakes. Embrace failure, even though it is hard for many people to do so. Fear of failure is the most important reason why many people do not try to do the things they want because they are afraid of making a fool of themselves. However, if you think that challenging ourselves will help strengthen us and learn from both our success stories and failures, you will be ready to embark on any journey you wish to without having to worry about the ending.

By embracing your mistakes you will take out the fear factor and be free to make your choices in accordance with your problem-solving skills. Challenging yourself little by little on a regular basis will help you built your confidence and personality. You could start by learning a new skill or taking up the hobby you wished to do for so long. Do everything in your power to succeed in both the skill and hobby you love. Push your limits a little more every time and enhance your curiosity about what will happen when you succeed. If you do not succeed, you will gain the necessary knowledge and insight to try again and this time avoid the mistakes you did previously.

Listening to our bodies will be an easy thing to do by following everything we have analyzed so far. Before you start practicing the methods that will enable you to succeed in this goal you have set, you should always keep in mind that positivity is the right perspective of which we should view life. Negativity never helped anyone and caused harm to the people who decided to give in to it. According to Kendra Cherry, author of Very Well Mind, the definition of positivity is,

"Positive thinking actually means approaching life's challenges with a positive outlook. It does not necessarily mean avoiding or ignoring the bad things; instead, it involves making the most of the potentially bad situations, trying to see the best in other people, and viewing yourself and your abilities in a positive light."

So, acknowledge that bit everything in life will go as you have planned them and be willing to make any effort necessary to realize your dreams even if you don't think they will pay off. Appreciate the good things life has to offer and grasp the opportunity you are given to develop a connection with your body. Do not forget that a positive attitude is considered the key to success because if you give in to pessimism and negativity you are surrendering your control to your emotions and will wallow in misery since you will be missing out an important opportunity you are given in leading a happy life through growth and development.

You want your body to respond to the connection you are trying to build with it in a positive way that will help you remain healthy for many years to come. If you approach this connection while maintaining negative emotions, it may as well shut you out and take the cue from you and be less resilient and strong. Optimism when forging a connection with your body will reduce the chances of you developing depression and high levels of stress as well as bring you the happiness so many people crave to attain.

Chapter 17: Mindfulness Meditation To Deal With Anxiety

We all experience feeling anxious every now and then. It is completely natural to feel anxious when thinking about something, which matters to us. The problem, however, lies in the habits that cause you to feel anxious for longer periods of time, to the point where it causes the quality of your life to suffer.

According to Psychiatrists, an anxiety disorder is having a relatively permanent state of nervousness and worry that occurs in varying degrees. In some cases, it leads to a panic attack or compulsive behavior that can harm the person affected and those around him or her. If you feel that your anxiety is no longer within your control, and if you believe that you are no longer living the kind of life you want because of it, then you must seek professional help.

However, if you know for a fact that you are still in control and you have the confidence to overcome your anxiety, then mindfulness meditation can help you deal with it. It may sound crazy to think that acknowledging anxiety will help you address it, but when you face the problem instead of fleeing from it, you have a higher chance of overcoming it.

It will also do you a lot of good to practice mindfulness meditation techniques, such as sitting meditation and mindful breathing meditation, during times when you are **not** experiencing anxiety. That way, you can condition your body and mind to be more open to relaxing and be more involved in the present moment, rather than ruminating over factors beyond your control.

Guided Mindfulness Meditation to Deal with Anxiety

The best way to apply mindfulness in order to deal with anxiety is through guided meditation. Guided meditation is when you are listening to a recorded voice of a meditation guru or teacher as you meditate. Through guided meditation, you can rely on the guru's voice to help you observe your thoughts in a more confident, rational and non-judgmental way.

There are plenty of free guided mindfulness meditation recordings online. You can also find a lot of free apps for all the major computer, tablet and phone brands that you can download.

However, if do not have access to them, then you can have a trusted friend read to you the following steps so that you can listen to his or her voice as you meditate:

Step 1: Sit comfortably and gently close your eyes.

Step 2: Take a slow, deep breath in then gently breathe it out. Take another deep breath in, and again, breathe it out.

Step 3: Continue to take in deep breaths. Inhale and take in the happiness, light, and peace of the universe. Exhale and breathe out the sadness, heaviness, and worry. Take your time to inhale all the goodness in, and exhale all the worries out.

Step 4: Begin to breathe as you normally would, without effort. Focus on your breath as the air enters through your nostrils, goes down your windpipe, and fills up your lungs. Notice how your lungs push the air back up through the windpipe and out of your nostrils.

Continue to breathe normally and focus more on your breath.

Step 5: Gently bring your focus towards your mind. Be curious and open towards the thoughts your mind is creating. Observe without any criticism. Become aware of the thoughts that cause you to feel anxious.

Honestly acknowledge the emotion you are feeling. You can say to yourself, "I am feeling anxious."

Step 6: Notice how your mind moves towards scenes or words that cause you to feel anxious. Observe them but stay detached. As you encounter a worrisome thought, say to yourself, "this is a thought", and then let it drift by. Repeat this with every thought.

Step 7: After labeling all the thoughts that came across your mind as what they are – thoughts – you can softly draw your focus back towards your breath. Each time a worrisome thought comes back, again label it as "a thought" and focus back to your breath.

Continue to focus on your breath until you feel more calm and relaxed then gently come out of the meditative state and allow yourself to rest for a few minutes before moving on with your day.

By practicing this regularly, you will realize that your thoughts are not your reality. Instead, the true reality is the present moment, where you are alive and in control of your behavior. By becoming aware of your anxiety and the presence of your worrisome thoughts, you can approach the stressful situation in a calm and collective manner.

You will also learn to interpret whether a worry is rational or irrational, and whether you have control over it or not. When you do, you no longer become overwhelmed by your anxiety. Instead, you learn to take charge of the things you can control and accept those that you cannot.

Chapter 18: A Step Forward To A Happier Life

What does true happiness mean to you? Is it possessing the things you've always wanted? A successful career in your chosen field? Being with the people you love most? Or simply rubbing the belly of your dog or cat? Each and every one of us has our own concept of what happiness truly means.

All of us wants to be happy and to feel joy in our lives. However, the challenges that we encounter along the way and the burdens we carry on our shoulders most of the times make it tough to achieve. As we continue our journey on this planet, these things are inevitable. We just have to think that the harder the situation is, the stronger we become – and mold into a better human being. Yes, it may be easier said than done, but your mentality changes the way you look and react. The universe is like a magnet, if your thoughts are filled with positivity, then good things often come your way, but if one is negativity, then a sequence of unfavorable turnouts can emerge through the surface. It sounds cliché, but it would be best if you ponder that the glass is always half full – meaning, start being an optimist. This way, you'll be able to attract encouraging circumstances to your life, and it may also be a gift you could bestow upon others.

Mandy Hale once said that "Happiness is letting go of what you think your life is supposed to look like and celebrating it for everything that it is." This is a brilliant and inspiring quote to live by. There's that point in our lives where we think that we've hit rock bottom, and it urges us to surrender. We tend to punish ourselves for the mistakes and failures we have made in the past. Hence we forget to appreciate what's happening now. The visions that we have set for our lives to become may not always become a reality.

Letting go is not easy all the time, but the key to it is acceptance and hardcore optimism. We have to accept that there are things that we can't change especially the ones that already belong to history, but you can certainly learn from it

There are a lot of books, blogs and personal experiences that could help inspire you to stay positive. Your everyday experiences can be used as lessons. Still, it's necessary to look at the world in a brighter perspective. Be with people who inspires you to bring out your best and never let one failure define who you are. Others may not see the great person you are. Just move on with your life and let them be.

Living a healthy lifestyle also helps you to feel good, and when you feel good inside, your aura oozes with radiance. Live life to the fullest and never let time pass you by without doing anything for yourself. You deserve a break from all the hate and negativity. Did you know that a 30-minute morning exercise can boost your mood for the entire day? Yes, you read that right. Research has shown that moving your body before going to work, school or even staying at home can help you set a feel-good spirit throughout the day. It'll jump start your day to make your more productive in everything you do. Exercise not because other people tell you to do so, but because you want to better yourself. As you move your bones and muscles, shift your thoughts and be as enthusiastic as you are.

A step forward to a healthier life can be challenging, but as you continue to walk the extra mile, you'll find it worth it in the end. In the long run, it will get easier, and you'll feel lighter. Don't ever underestimate your capabilities to make a change and stand up for what true happiness means.

Yoga and You: 5 S' That'll Surprise You And Turn Your Life Around

Leading a healthy life can mean a happy life. Getting yourself moving can provide you with the energy that you need every day. We have mentioned previously that there are a lot of exercises you can do to help achieve a healthier lifestyle and one of which is Yoga.

Stress in just one of the major factors that contribute to an unhappy life. When you are stressed, you can easily get irritated. Stress can make you extermly angry or frustrated. It can affect your productivity at work and your mood inside your household. Almost everything around you is affected. Let me reiterate that Yoga can help reduce stress levels which are significant.

Considering Yoga as part of your life can make a huge impact on how to perceive and interpret the things that are happening around you. Yoga's benefits to a happier life can be more surprising than you think. Ultimately, here are five advantages Yoga can add to your welfare.

Self-Esteem

Yoga helps you become fit. When you feel good about how you look, self-esteem and confidence start to build. With exercises and routines, you'll be fully aware of what you're capable of and determine your limitations. Having self-esteem builds a personality with little fear. It allows you to get rid of negativity that lurks inside your head and helps you will feel peacefulness, and strength.

The meditation exercises of yoga can help you understand that you are whom you are. You need to live with yourself. You can improve yourself, and your body. However you must live with yourself. This is the concept that limitations are not downfalls, but simply who and what you are. Once you have accepted the things that you can and can't do, your self-confidence will intensify.

It can also strengthen your mind to believe in yourself and what you are capable of. No matter what challenge comes your way, you will be confident enough to face it. Having self-confidence can make you care less of what other people think about you

Soulful Existence

Yoga helps fight the signs of stress and moderate its levels. Aside from that, its meditation exercises allow you to reach the inner cores of your mind and spirit. You'll learn how to live in the moment and appreciate the true meaning of your life.

Yoga allows you to recognize the good things and keep you mindful of what's happening around you. It gives you the benefit of seeing your positive value, hence, transforms you into a rejuvenated and recharged person – a better version of yourself. Your mind and approach to life may gain some flexibility as well.

Holistic healing can change a person, and it will certainly provide you a happier life. It encourages you to do, think and speak good things with people that surround you. Given this, you allow goodness to enter your life, thus, generously give portions of it to your fellow men. Forgiving easily, letting go of futile stuff that doesn't matter. Meaning, you're just not merely living to survive, but you exist with greater sense. You're living a higher purpose in this world, and you would feel the fulfillment from within knowing that you have done the right thing.

Standpoint

Meditation and breathing exercises of Yoga work wonder on your mind, body and spirit – a holistic healing. This allows better outlook and understanding of things. Feeling good inside can calm and relax your mind. This can make room for positive things to happen. It allows your mind to retreat from your hectic lifestyle.

Yoga attracts positivity helping you to see the brighter side of life no matter how obscure the road may be. It cleanses your mind from negative thoughts and makes out the journey's right destination as well as the way leading to it. Optimistic people tend to have favorable views towards the world. Being positive can help people to be more productive, be brighter, and keep that 'feel good' vibe which can influence a good physical and mental health.

It's fulfilling to know that you are looking at the world in a different point of view. You're not only helping yourself but others as well. You can be their candle in the night, a guide that leads to them through the dark. A positive standpoint can lift you higher, and you'll be surprised how much you can achieve. Plus, it can kindle the spirit within you to never surrender and just focus on your goal.

Success

When you accomplish a task or a goal, normally, you call it a success, right? And it makes you happy knowing that you did your best to do it. Success has many forms, and it depends on how you perceive it to be. However, no matter what success means to you, Yoga will be there to guide you.

The other S advantages that we have mentioned previously are interconnected to each other, especially to success. When you have self-esteem, positive standpoint and soulful existence, you are most likely to succeed in life. Why? It is because you can handle stress better and you are more enthusiastic in everything you do. Yoga can help you focus on what's important and disregard negative thoughts as you move along. You possess patience on your task because you have a calm and relaxed mind. Yoga exercises work its magic in building your body to be ready for your life's journey.

Yoga Meditation exercise is all about relaxing a busy mind, directing you to live and experience each moment to the fullest. So, once you achieve something, even how simple it is, the joy you can feel deep in your heart is indescribable. Especially if you lifted other people along in your success. Seeing them happy and celebrating your success with them, that's more success than you could ever hope for – that's called life fulfillment.

Sex

Yes, you read it right. Yoga can help you achieve a better and happier sex life. Aside from the physical improvement, Yoga exercises also help the release of endorphins, which are called the "feel-good" hormones of our body, allowing us to be happy, and feel less pain. Studies have shown that Yoga can lowers stress levels. This can make you in the mood more often and less likely to argue with your significant other. Also, yoga involves engaging and drawing up the muscles of the pelvic area, which strengthens the muscles that play an integral role in sex. It is clear that yoga can boost athletic performance, but Yoga also helps when it comes to making love. Some studies have indicated that Yoga exercise can also be advantageous when it comes to making act of love making more satisfying. Its physical benefits sanction you to be more flexible in bed, especially in performing different sexual positions. The outcome will be an increase in sexual desire as well as sexual gratification. Additionally, it is believed that by marginally contracting the coccygeal pub muscles can heighten arousal and amend sexual performance. All this is possible by a remote muscle contraction phenomenon that composes an energetic seal that locks breath in our body, which then carries circulation and information to the pelvic region.

Moreover, regular practice helps to strengthen, lengthen and tone your body, and all of these will make you feel better about yourself. Thus, it will boost your self-confidence. that will help you feel more sexy and comfortable with another body beside you.

Life

There are a lot of reasons to celebrate life and be happy with what is happening at present. There may be bumps in the road, but the path will never change. You just have to keep going and don't lose yourself along the way. Live life as it is, and as long as you embody the teachings of Yoga, you should always expect the unexpected. For you'll never know when another surprise shall arrive at the right moment. Despite the fact that some of the things we want are insatiable, our overall being can still be satisfied if holistic healing has taken its toll and make us aware of the things that truly matter in this world – Things that are more than what meets the naked eye.

Techniques To Achieve Inner Peace

Inner peace probably is the most difficult condition to achieve. No matter how hard we try most of the time, a lot of the time we don't pay attention to events or situations that occur around us. The intensity of the situation can hurt us, and we tend to react to it in an adverse manner. Sometimes, it's easier to convince ourselves that we have peace and that what others think about us is none of our business, yet, subconsciously, we think about it. It's like we're pretending to make the situation better, or so it seems, but the fact is, it makes it even harder to overcome.

Conclusion

Thank you again for downloading and reading this book!

I hope that these tips about mindfulness and stress management offered you some outlook on life! This book provided some straightforward and essential strategies that you can utilize to be able to live in the present, forget about your past, and put away all your future worries. All of these strategies you might have taken for granted, ignoring the fact of how powerful and life changing they really are. Implement these strategies in your life, and you will immediately see a huge shift in the direction of your life. You will feel as though all the stress and worry has been taken off your shoulders and be able to live a genuinely happier and meaningful life.

More importantly, a less stressful life is a healthier life. When you start focusing on joy and happiness instead of stress and anxiety, you will notice a vast improvement in your health. So, go on and work towards this habit of mindfulness and living in the present. Apply all the ideas and strategies as soon as you can. You don't need to wait for the perfect moment to take action. Now is always the best time to shape your perspective and live life to the fullest!

www.ingramcontent.com/pod-product-compliance
Lightning Source LLC
Chambersburg PA
CBHW072014070526
44583CB00015B/1479